W9-AIK-488

FINANCIAL
ARMAGEDDON

JOHN HAGEE

FRONT LINE

A STRANG COMPANY

Most STRANG COMMUNICATIONS/CHARISMA HOUSE/CHRISTIAN LIFE/EXCEL BOOKS/ FRONTLINE/REALMS/SILOAM products are available at special quantity discounts for bulk purchase for sales promotions, premiums, fund-raising, and educational needs. For details, write Strang Communications Book Group, 600 Rinehart Road, Lake Mary, Florida 32746, or telephone (407) 333-0600.

FINANCIAL ARMAGEDDON by John Hagee
Published by FrontLine, a Strang company
600 Rinehart Road, Lake Mary, Florida 32746
www.strangdirect.com

Unless otherwise noted, all Scripture quotations are from the New King James Version of the Bible. Copyright © 1979, 1980, 1982 by Thomas Nelson, Inc., publishers. Used by permission.

Scripture quotations marked AMP are from the Amplified Bible. Old Testament copyright © 1965, 1987 by the Zondervan Corporation. The Amplified New Testament copyright © 1954, 1958, 1987 by the Lockman Foundation. Used by permission.

Scripture quotations marked KJV are from the King James Version of the Bible.

Scripture quotations marked NAS are from the New American Standard Bible. Copyright © 1960, 1962, 1963, 1968, 1971, 1972, 1973, 1975, 1977 by the Lockman Foundation. Used by permission.

Scripture quotations marked NIV are from the Holy Bible, New International Version. Copyright © 1973, 1978, 1984, International Bible Society. Used by permission.

Scripture quotations marked NLT are from the Holy Bible, New Living Translation, copyright © 1996, 2004. Used by permission of Tyndale House Publishers, Inc., Wheaton, IL 60189. All rights reserved.

Design Director: Bill Johnson; Cover design by Justin Evans

Library of Congress Cataloging-in-Publication Data:
Hagee, John.
  Financial Armageddon / John Hagee. -- 1st ed.
       p. cm.
  Includes bibliographical references.
  ISBN 978-1-59979-603-1
  1. Economics in the Bible. 2. Bible--Prophecies--Armageddon. 3. Finance, Personal--Biblical teaching. 4. Armageddon--Biblical teaching. I. Title.
  BS670.H27 2008
  261.8'5--dc22

                                    2008044034

First Edition

09 10 11 12 13 — 10 9 8 7 6 5 4 3
Printed in the United States of America

Contents

Foreword

THE FINANCIAL CRISIS THAT DEVELOPED ON WALL STREET in the fall of 2008 is unlike anything I've seen before in my career. No one seems to have the answers, even though everyone is trying to figure out what the crisis means.

Financial Armageddon by Pastor John Hagee provides answers from the Word of God. Hagee is a powerful minister whose preaching and teaching put difficult times into perspective for Christians, and he has great insight into the meaning of current events from a biblical perspective. For example, when oil prices skyrocketed in mid-2008, Hagee prepared a teaching series titled "The Oil Crisis and the Road to Armageddon." The response to the series was more than double what is usually expected. Why? Because people want answers, and Hagee gives them.

I believe the existing crisis is so important that I encouraged our Strang Book Group to rush this book into print. It appeared on bookstore shelves only six weeks after we conceived the idea—a time frame that is almost unheard of in publishing circles.

The problems we are currently experiencing have a greater significance than a typical credit crunch or mortgage crisis. They are a precursor to a tremendous battle that will take place at what the Bible calls *Armageddon*. (See Revelation 16:14, 16.) In order to understand them, we must learn to discern the times, as the sons of Issachar did in 1 Chronicles 12:32, and view them in light of the Word of God.

As a businessman, I read Hagee's manuscript with great interest. What happens on Wall Street or in international markets affects me and those who work with me. Plus, I have some investments in the stock market for my retirement years, and I don't want to see them wiped out. Whether you own a business as I do or work for someone else, I know you too want to understand what is going on.

Let me add my perspective to what you're about to read, and

maybe I can help you comprehend something about what the media sometimes hysterically call *a financial meltdown*.

The stock market has plummeted before, and I believe it will recover. So I'm not planning to revamp my stock portfolio. I expect the value of the stocks to increase in the future. I still remember the dot-com bubble that burst a few years ago, the recession of 1992, and the terrible "stagflation" of the 1970s when I was just beginning my career.

Our current situation has come as no surprise. Considering some of the bad loans that were made, the *creative instruments* Wall Street created, and the overblown real estate market, it was only a matter of time until something drastic happened to correct the mistakes. But the panic that has set in has made the problems worse, even though our federal government has spent billions of dollars to try to stabilize the market.

I think we can expect that America will come out of this bear market and financial slump just as it has before. But every time we experience a downturn, people want our government to do more. Year by year we become more of an international market, depending on international banks to help stabilize the financial situation. If this doesn't occur, people panic.

When people panic, they look for a strong leader who will give them what they want and make their financial problems go away. Do you see the pattern that develops? A global economy and global crises make people yearn for a global leader to solve their problems. Suddenly you have the scenario the Bible says leads to the rise of a man called the Antichrist, who leads us into the Battle of Armageddon!

If you don't think this is possible, look at history. It was the terrible inflation and financial problems after World War I in Germany that made the people turn to Hitler. Not only *could* it happen again, but, according to the Bible, it *will* happen again.

That's why it's important to understand what is going on. All of us are at risk because we live in a complex, world-financial system that causes us to be dependent on others to provide the groceries we buy and to deliver the gas we put in our cars. We are dependent on others to have the money to buy the goods and services we sell or to pay our paychecks. When any part of the system breaks down, we are vulnerable like everyone else. Period.

So we must do what we can not only to survive but also to thrive in difficult economic situations such as the current bear market on Wall Street, which may be part of the bigger financial Armageddon that is coming.

The first step is to rein in our fear. Financial crisis can lead to collapse simply because people become afraid and panic. We must understand that God's Word is true whether stocks are up or down and whether credit is tight or abundant.

Long before President Franklin D. Roosevelt, in his 1933 inaugural address, said in reference to the depressed economic condition of our nation, "The only thing we have to fear is fear itself,"[1] God Himself had given us the admonition not to fear. He said through the prophet Isaiah, "'Fear not, for I have redeemed you.... When you pass through the waters, I will be with you; and through the rivers, they shall not overflow you. When you walk through the fire, you shall not be burned, nor shall the flame scorch you.... Since you were precious in My sight, you have been honored, and I have loved you" (Isa. 43:1–4).

Next we must understand that there are different levels of economic problems. The first is a normal negative cycle in the markets. Such cycles come and go, and things usually get better. But at the same time, they set us up for a greater danger, what author Larry Bates calls "the new economic disorder," in which world banks control the money, cartels control oil, and evil leaders set the scenario for the coming Antichrist.[2]

When Armageddon comes, no one will escape it, because world events will crash together with biblical prophecy in the final conflict of the ages, as Pastor Hagee explains in these pages. Yet there is hope for believers who understand that the Rapture will take away Christians "in the twinkling of an eye."

Of course, it's that knowledge that has also led generations of Christians to be passive and simply wait for the Second Coming to whisk them away from all the troubles of the world. Their attitude is like that of the preacher who joked, "It's easier to think about the 'sweet by-and-by' than it is to deal with the nasty now-and-now."

Maybe the problems we're experiencing will wake up the church. Maybe godly leaders will emerge in government and the economic community to provide answers based on the principles of God's Word that will change the tide or at least slow it down.

Some Christians in the world—believers in the Sudan, Communist China, or India, where there has been so much violence against Christians, or in the Muslim world, where Christianity is banned—may think Armageddon has already begun. Americans, on the other hand, believe they are somehow immune. They think, "Surely these problems won't happen to us." We've been blessed with relative peace and prosperity so long we believe they are our rights. Yet bad things can happen and are happening. As the leader of the free world, America is not exempt.

Consider 9/11. We never thought we would be attacked on our own soil, but we were. I believe many other events that have been prophesied will take place, and we can only prepare.

As people the world over become more and more hostile to the gospel, and as those who are evil get into power and take away our freedoms, Christians must do what the Jews did in Europe, where they were persecuted for years—engage in professions and trades we can take with us when things get bad. The trend that developed during those years explains why many Jews are in banking, jewelry, and so on rather than farming today.

So what can Christians do? Start businesses. Get involved in the process to change things rather than being subject to the whims of big business.

Then run your small business in a way that can handle a downturn. Have reserves; keep debt low; make fallback plans. In the process, be able to help others as the Bible says.

Too often Christians, like the men Moses sent to spy out the Promised Land (Num. 13:32–33), have seen themselves as grasshoppers in their own eyes—in this case, as being at the bottom of the economic totem pole just waiting for the Rapture. This image is not accurate, and the Bible has answers for the mess we're in. That's why John Hagee's book is so important. Read it and share it with friends. Follow the advice he gives.

Remember that, no matter what happens, we are to do as the nobleman in the Bible instructed his servants, and "occupy till [our Master] come[s]" (Luke 19:13, KJV).

—Stephen Strang
Founder and Publisher of *Charisma*

Chapter 1

WHAT IS GOING ON?

F*INANCIAL ARMAGEDDON* WILL REVEAL THE INTERSECTION of our current global economic crisis with Bible prophecy. If you have turned your television on in the past two months or read a newspaper, you already know that America is facing an economic crisis that many are saying is similar to what happened in America just before the Great Depression. One financial institution after another has crumbled. Mammoth mortgage brokers Freddie Mac and Fannie Mae led the way.

With Wall Street financial markets plummeting, Congress recently approved a $700 billion bailout package that could become the most expensive government intervention in history.[1] Many Americans believe it is nothing more than a Band-Aid that could lead to more financial debt and ultimately bring financial collapse to average Americans.

When our national media aired the decision of Congress to approve this bailout, foreign markets, economists, and politicians were unable to agree on much of anything about what this meant to global economics. But on October 8, 2008, the Federal Reserve, along with the European Central Bank and the central banks of the United Kingdom, Canada, Switzerland, and Sweden, cut interest rates in response to the global credit crunch that pushed borrowing costs to record levels and forced governments across Europe to bail out banks.[2]

Such unprecedented worldwide events are prophesied in the Word of God. In *Financial Armageddon* I will show you how the converging worldwide oil crisis plays a major role in prophetic end-of-the-age events—indeed, paves the road to the great Battle of Armageddon. For the first time in history, all the major players in the Bible's prophecy are on the stage that leads to the final conflict of the ages.

I will also reveal God's secrets for avoiding a personal economic crash. The current economic crisis in America—and the world—has heightened the concerns and fears of every American. One of the first questions people ask when any crisis hits is: "Why didn't someone see this coming?" The second question, following right on the heels of the first, is: "What do I do now?" Certainly, in the face of what seems to be an economic crisis that happened overnight, you may be asking these questions now.

Let me assure you that America's current economic position didn't happen overnight. *We did see this coming.* It has been brewing for several years, and many conservative economists have been predicting this very thing. For example, in 2003 Christian economist Larry Bates made this statement:

> The peaks and valleys, booms and busts, in the economy, all those "opportunities to profit," are actually the result of deliberate policy actions by policy makers in the government and the Federal Reserve. Simply put, there is a small group of people in this country and around the world who have the resources and the power to determine the direction our economy will take.[3]

Bates identified "five powerful, dangerous and unstoppable forces that will soon hit our economy with the force of a runaway train." These included:

1. The banking crisis
2. Federal debts and deficits
3. Business and personal debt
4. Recession/depression
5. Massive, renewed inflation[4]

It's pretty obvious to even the most uninformed American that predictions like those Bates made have, indeed, come true.

But I want you to understand something even more important than the predictions made by any economist—even a Christian one. Our Master Investment Counselor—God—has not only predicted everything that is going to happen in the world, including global finances, *but He has also given us the only tool we need to answer the second question: "What do I do now?"*

I believe that we are witnessing world events converging with biblical prophecy that will usher us into the appearing of the Antichrist and, seven years later, the second coming of Christ. Ancient Bible prophets spoke of these events by saying, "This is what the LORD Almighty says: 'In a little while I will once more shake the heavens and the earth, the sea and the dry land. I will shake all nations, and the desired of all nations will come'" (Hag. 2:6–7, NIV).

Economists and financial analysts—Christian and non-Christian alike—are predicting a "new world order" like what was prophesied in God's Word. One analyst said recently, "The United States is leading the world into a 'new world order' where financial systems will be taken over by governments and coordinated by a central committee of the ruling elite."[5]

And national and international media are reporting these events as they happen, as with the recent headline news about the coordinating efforts of the Fed and other central banks to cut interest rates.[6]

Christians throughout this nation, along with other Americans, are worried about how these cataclysmic events are going to affect their families and pocketbooks. In an atmosphere of fear, it is our natural tendency to worry and expect the worst. That's why I've written this book. I want you to understand that now—as in every other moment of history—God is in control. He knew this was going to happen. He knows what will happen next. And He knows what you can do about it.

The second chapter of this book is foundational to the entire book. It paints a panoramic picture of what has happened and why it is happening, and—more importantly—it helps us to see what is yet to come. Don't miss reading it!

In the first section of this book, we will take a closer look at the world events that have led to where we are today. But even more important, we will discover what is behind the crisis and see how Bible prophecy predicts what will happen next. We will look at the current conflict in the Middle East over oil. We will consider the rise—and fall—of America and see how nations around the world are becoming world players in events that will lead to the final conflict of the ages.

In section two we will take a closer look at the intersection between Bible prophecy and world events. You will see that in God's eyes, the nation of Israel is the center of the world. You will understand the importance of Israel's threat from Iran and see how the formation of the European Union parallels a rebirth of the Roman Empire. As we end this section, you will have the opportunity to find answers to critical questions you should be asking.

In the third section of this book, we will look at what our Master Investment Counselor says regarding our personal financial security in the face of threatening economic collapse. I want you to understand the danger of debt and the need to choose giving over hoarding in response to economic threats. You can be assured that with God's help, you can avoid the pitfalls brought on by the economic crisis facing the world today.

I will reveal to you what God—your Master Investment Counselor—says about the things that you see happening daily. And I'll help you to understand what God wants you to do to protect your family and possessions from crumbling in financial devastation.

As you read this book, remember that God is in control. He has promised:

> For I know the thoughts that I think toward you, says the LORD, thoughts of peace and not of evil, to give you a future and a hope.
>
> —JEREMIAH 29:11

Chapter 2

AMERICA'S ECONOMIC MELTDOWN: THE PERFECT STORM

IN THIS CHAPTER, WE WILL DISCOVER HOW OUR GLOBAL economic crisis reveals a panorama of things to come.[1] In the past quarter century, the United States has witnessed unparalleled economic growth. During this period, the nation gained forty million jobs, the Dow Jones moved from eight hundred to over fourteen thousand, and the world saw a significant reduction in poverty.[2]

However, by the end of Friday, October 10, 2008, the Dow ended its worst week in history, dropping over 18 percent in just five days. Even more troubling, from its high one year earlier, the Dow was down over 40 percent. Another stock market indicator, the S&P 500, was down over 42 percent.[3] One estimate suggested that more than $7 trillion in shareholder value had been wiped out.[4]

In the two previous years, more than one million people had lost their homes, with another million expected to lose them in the coming year.[5] One scholar believes it is conceivable we could see a total drop of 25 percent in housing prices, comparable to the Great Depression.[6] Former Federal Reserve chairman Paul Volcker has said, "We are in the midst of the worst financial turmoil since the Great Depression."

We are not there yet. Unemployment during that period hit

25 percent, far worse than the current 6 percent, and the nation experienced sharp drops in GDP (gross domestic product), something the nation has yet to see in 2008. Nevertheless, banks have failed, the federal government is taking direct control of large parts of the American economy, and political leaders are promising large tax hikes in response to the crisis.[7] Comparisons to the 1930s are becoming more common and have even entered the political debate.

The United States has experienced banking crises before in its history. Earlier examples include 1797, 1819, 1837, 1857, 1873, 1893, 1907, 1929, and 1987.[8] The question is: What caused the current financial crisis? This chapter will outline the causes of our current problems, connecting those causes to other aspects of the American and world economic systems.

HOW THE FINANCIAL CRISIS EVOLVED

The current financial crisis was caused by the real estate bubble that began in the late 1990s, but it is connected and linked to a variety of other factors. In an effort to clarify the story, I will treat each factor in turn, but it is important to recognize that these various elements are all interconnected.

Subprime lending

A central aspect of the public philosophy in the United States is home ownership. One scholar calls it a "national obsession."[9] Home ownership is perceived as an integral part of the American dream, and public policy is geared to promote it. The federal income tax code is structured to encourage home ownership, and it has been a key aspect of electoral politics. This philosophy became so powerful that in 1977 Congress passed, and President Jimmy Carter signed into law, the Community Reinvestment Act (CRA), which declared that banks have "an affirmative obligation" to meet the credit needs of the communities in which they are chartered. When banks were later accused of discriminating against poor and minority neighborhoods, the Clinton administration tightened the regulations on banks to encourage them to invest more money in higher-risk areas.

The federal government also encourages home ownership through the Federal National Mortgage Association (Fannie Mae) and the Federal Home Loan Mortgage Corporation (Freddie Mac). Fannie Mae was established during the Great Depression, while Freddie Mac was created in 1970 to provide competition to Fannie Mae. Although the two companies eventually became publicly traded companies, the federal government heavily regulates them, and their charters require them to promote home ownership among lower-income and disadvantaged groups.[10] In this sense, home ownership for the poor is seen by some as a key civil rights issue, and both President Bill Clinton and President George W. Bush pushed home ownership as a matter of policy.

None of this explains why things got out of hand. How did a philosophy of home ownership become a real estate bubble that burst?

As recently as the early 1980s, mortgage rates were as high as 18 percent. By 2003 they had declined to just over 5 percent. In the interim, several important things happened. In the 1990s, China began to rise in importance as an economic powerhouse. Manufacturing in China began to flood the world with cheap products, which helped to keep inflation low. This allowed central banks, such as the Federal Reserve in the United States, to keep interest rates very low.

Deflation, not inflation, was a major concern. When the tech-stock bubble collapsed in 2000, leading to the relatively mild recession of 2001, investors looked for a place to put their money. That place was real estate.[11]

For most of the century prior to 1997, home prices had not changed very much. When adjusted for inflation, prices varied slightly within a fairly narrow band. But in the late 1990s, a housing boom took off. From 1997 to 2006, real home prices increased 85 percent.[12] Home sales rose and prices rose, causing building construction to rise for all sorts of reasons. Some buyers simply wanted to take advantage of the boom to renovate or remodel their homes. Others wanted to refinance to gain greater wealth. Some used the opportunity to trade up to a higher-quality home. First-time buyers sought to grab a piece of the American dream.

One of the things that made this massive level of activity possible was the existence of subprime loans. *Subprime loans* are loans made to individuals who have a weak or troubled credit history.[13] *Prime borrowers* are people who have a good history of debt repayment. *Subprime borrowers* are people who either have problems with debt repayment or who have no credit history at all. With official government policy encouraging home ownership for as many people as possible, incentives existed for lending institutions to provide new loan products for people with shaky credit histories—especially those from poor or minority neighborhoods, the prime target of Fannie Mae and Freddie Mac.

Policy makers, including Federal Reserve chairman Alan Greenspan, encouraged the development and use of subprime loans. In 2006, 90 percent of subprime loans came in the form of adjustable rate mortgages (ARMs). Fixed-rate mortgages, the more traditional form of financing homes, lock in monthly payments that never change. ARMs typically start at an interest rate lower than fixed-rate loans but reset after a period of time to match a specific interest rate benchmark. Rates may adjust as often as every six months, up or down depending on the interest rate. Other vehicles used to encourage home ownership included little to no down payments, minimal or nonexistent proof of income, and even *stated income* loans in which the borrower simply states his income and the lender accepts that number without proof.[14] In short, lenders who should have known better were giving loans to people purchasing homes they could not afford.

All of this activity might have been fine had housing prices continued to rise. However, scholars analyzing this situation agreed that a bubble psychology took shape in the global economy. People began to believe we were in a new era in which prices would never come down, at least not nationally. In a new era of *riskless risk*, people began to think that home prices would stay high permanently.[15]

The housing boom turned into a bubble when people began to think of housing not as a means to buy a home but as an investment. With the tech-stock bubble gone and low interest rates, what can we do with our money? So, investors sought a piece of the action, as did speculators who bought and sold properties quickly for a profit. Banks took advantage of the situation to seek higher profits by making riskier bets. Instead of banks holding a mortgage for the life of the loan, banks began to collect all of the loans, including risky subprime loans, into a single pool; then they divided this pool into separate pieces to sell to a global market.[16]

The ride came to an abrupt end in 2006. As housing prices continued to rise, housing construction boomed. Eventually prices got too high, and overpriced homes began to fall in value. When adjustable-rate mortgages had their rates reset, people suddenly found they could not afford to make their payments. Home owners saw three hundred fifty dollars per month added to their house payment. The result was the beginning of an era of bankruptcies and foreclosures that has yet to end. Home owners soon owed more on their loans than their houses were worth. Prices came crashing down, with the drop felt in all sectors of the country and at all price tiers, as well as overseas.[17]

Far worse, banking institutions were caught flat-footed. Bad subprime loans had been divided into many smaller parts and spread throughout the world's financial system, and all of a sudden those investment vehicles were bad. No one knew exactly where these assets were, and the result was a panic and loss of faith and trust in the system. This led to a reevaluation of risk in general. After all, if mortgages were overvalued, so might be all kinds of other assets. This is how the bundling of mortgages, comprising only $200 billion in a multitrillion-dollar global economy, could cause banks in other countries to go under.[18]

The result in 2008 is now well known. The housing crash and ensuing loss of confidence in the credit markets caused the investment firm Bear Stearns to lose access to credit in March. At that time, the federal government chose to intervene and rescue Bear Stearns by facilitating its sale to JPMorgan Chase. Congress gave the Treasury Department authority to take over Fannie Mae and Freddie Mac in July, and the Treasury nationalized those two entities on September 8.

On September 15, Lehman Brothers took the honors for the largest bankruptcy filing in American history. The following day, the Federal Reserve made a loan to shore up American International Group (AIG), the largest insurance company in the world. All of these firms had trouble securing financing because of the housing crash, due primarily to bad subprime loans. As financial institutions throughout the world began to understand what had happened, the resulting loss of trust prompted them to stop lending to each other.

In the wake of these actions and the resulting stock market turmoil, the federal government is taking unprecedented actions to address the problem, including a $700 billion bailout plan for Wall Street and claiming part ownership of the largest banks to provide stability to the market.

Other factors

The relationship between subprime lending and the housing bubble was the principal cause of the current financial crisis, but there are related factors as well. For example, the role of the new Chinese economy cannot be overstated. China's emergence as an economic power in the 1990s helped force down prices for manufactured goods, leading the Federal Reserve to keep interest rates down to fight deflation. China's entry into the World Trade Organization (WTO) made it a low-cost place to produce goods, and China soon began producing more than 10 percent of the world's goods, adversely impacting industries in other countries. The resulting trade deficit meant foreign countries were investing heavily in U.S. Treasury bonds, as well as other items such as mortgage securities. Chinese demand and explosive growth also led to soaring oil prices, thus linking real estate speculation to speculation in energy. The surge in oil prices led to increasing investment in energy, including ethanol, which led in turn to a surge in food prices, creating tremendous problems in developing countries.[19]

Some scholars call attention to the potentially dangerous role China plays in the global economy. Potentially, China represents the next economic bubble. In its attempt to join market forces to a Marxist political system ripe with corruption and inefficiency, China is paving the way for problems at the global level. Its purchasing of commodities worldwide, including oil, indicates a similar psychology to the real estate bubble—no one believes it will burst. When it does, the consequences for the world will be deflation, global stock market collapse, and long-term stagnation.

The growing disproportionate male-female ratio in China, due to its one-child policy and common practice of aborting female babies, is creating a demographic nightmare that will only compound the problem. Alternatively, China could withdraw its reserves from the global system, leading to world inflation as central banks raise interest rates to compensate.[20] Such a move would seem unlikely.

A 2007 study found that no single nation holds enough U.S. debt to cause a major disruption, and taking such action would undermine the value of their own holdings, causing them to suffer huge losses.[21] Still, that prognosis depends on the assumption that nations will always act rationally, and the current subprime crisis demonstrates the folly of such an assumption.

Linked to both China and the real estate bubble is the role of foreign oil. In mid-2007, the price of oil was sixty-five dollars per barrel. One year later it had nearly doubled. Demand for oil by China helped raise the price, but American consumption of foreign oil played its own part. The housing crisis led to a drop in the dollar, creating another surge in oil, food, and commodity prices. The resulting high oil prices joined the subprime crisis in putting downward pressure on the dollar.

To put this problem in perspective, every penny increase in the price of a gallon of gas costs over one billion dollars in extra annual spending. The jump from three dollars per gallon to four dollars per gallon caused the nation's gas bill to rise more than $100 billion, rendering the federal government's

2008 stimulus checks nearly impotent. The potential for a free fall of the dollar and collapse of the economy is very real.[22]

Indirectly linked to the subprime crisis, but directly connected to its potential consequences, is the state of America's national debt. Before the Wall Street bailout package passed by Congress, the most obvious source of rising debt for the United States was from money spent to fight the war in Iraq, which over the past five years is rapidly nearing $600 billion. That may be dwarfed by the $700 billion bailout package and $250 billion government purchase of bank shares. The federal deficit for fiscal year 2008 is estimated at a record $455 billion, more than twice the amount of the 2007 budget deficit. Some analysts believe that fiscal year 2009 could see a deficit in excess of $700 billion.

Far more imposing on the future is the entitlement debt incurred by the United States. As the baby boom generation begins to move into retirement, we may see the Social Security and Medicare systems overloaded. Between 2000 and 2030, the sixty-five-year-old population will more than double in this country. The number of retirees will go from thirty-five million to seventy-two million—20 percent of the total population. The cost of Social Security, Medicare, and Medicaid will rise from $1.1 trillion and 40 percent of the federal budget today to more than $2 trillion and 75 percent of the federal budget in 2030.[23] Medicare Part A benefit payments should exceed revenue this year, and assets will not be sufficient to pay full benefits as early as 2019. Social Security payments will exceed revenue in 2017, and assets will not be sufficient to pay full benefits by 2041.

Total national debt—the interest on which constitutes an increasingly large percentage of the annual federal budget—now exceeds $9 trillion.[24] Perhaps most shocking, the true national debt—defined as all debt held in the United States, public and private—is $53 trillion. Common sense tells us that such a debt is unsustainable.

CONSEQUENCES OF THE FINANCIAL CRISIS

Although it is important not to exaggerate the consequences of the current financial crisis, it is critical that we understand where it could take us. The obvious consequences lie in the economic arena, should the crisis continue and worsen. If people suspect that they will lose their money, we could see a run on the banks. Banks keep only a fraction of deposited money on hand, and such a run would be devastating. The crisis that led to the Great Depression started before 1929 in the housing market.

Less apocalyptically, the country faces a real threat of recession. Demand for home construction will fall, which will affect employment and the economy. State and local public finances depend on property taxes, and the housing crash could negatively affect government finances. A falling dollar and renewed surge in oil and food prices will put pressure on the family budget, and a decline in home owners' net worth will make money for college that much more difficult to come by. Some households will see their nest eggs disappear, while others will no longer have access to credit.[25]

Internationally, we are already seeing the effects of the subprime crisis. Iceland has essentially gone bankrupt, forced to accept help from Russia and to once again consider possible membership in the European Union (EU), further expanding that body. The vigorous actions of national governments also raise the specter of moral hazard—bailing out risk takers with taxpayer money. This may be an understandable development since the crisis itself has its genesis in the lack of moral virtue—when working hard is seen as less important than shrewd investing, and irresponsible bankers and political leaders violate their trust.

The most profound and potentially far-reaching consequences may be political. Historically, economic crises have never been kind to the incumbent party in a presidential election year. Severe recession in the late 1830s called into question the stewardship of the economy by Jacksonian Democrats, allowing the Whig party to win control of both Congress and the White House for the only time in its history. The worst depression of the 1800s started in 1893 just as Grover Cleveland began his second term. Four bitter years later he surrendered the office to Republican William McKinley, who began a thirty-six-year dominance of national politics by the GOP. By 1932, however, Republican management of the economy had been discredited with the onset of the Great Depression, allowing Franklin Roosevelt to redefine American politics for the next few decades. Only the stagflation and foreign policy weakness of the Carter administration ended the New Deal era, paving the way for Ronald Reagan and modern conservatism.

This historical overview is important because the current financial crisis is being spoken of in terms comparing it to the Great Depression. It remains to be seen how bad things will get, but there is no question that the crisis has helped make Democratic presidential candidate Barack Obama the presumptive favorite and subsequent president-elect during the 2008 election, with the likelihood of a substantially stronger Democratic majority in both houses of Congress come January 2009, perhaps even a filibuster-proof majority in the Senate. If a strong election victory by Obama is interpreted as more than simply a desire to change management—if, instead, it is interpreted as a desire for a new public philosophy—then it is possible to argue that conservative free-market economic policies have been repudiated and the Reagan era has come to an end.[26]

What would that mean? Some scholars are already calling for action "on the scale of the New Deal–era reformers."[27] Such action would mean a shift away from free trade and entrepreneurialism in favor of protectionism and class warfare. A renewed emphasis on the redistribution of wealth would be joined to a preference for large, new federal programs, starting with a comprehensive health-care program. The response to the financial crisis will involve more government bailouts at all levels and further efforts to stimulate the economy. The promised tax cuts and programs for clean energy and jobs and infrastructure spending will create a deficit and debt problem seemingly impossible to address.[28]

And, of course, these domestic and economic issues will be

linked to liberal policies in national security and foreign policy, as well as social issues. A Democratic administration will likely be much more sympathetic to European sensibilities and will work diligently to coordinate actions and policies with the EU. It will be, in short, the return of big government.

The future is not yet set in stone, but history demonstrates that voters are remarkably unforgiving toward the party they hold responsible for economic disaster. The facts are much more complicated, of course, but facts are less relevant to voters who are angry.

SECTION I
OIL PAVES THE ROAD
TO ARMAGEDDON

Chapter 3

THE RISE AND FALL
OF AMERICA

Amerika is facing a series of major crises. We are facing a crisis of leadership in America, and the world is now searching for a new *Caesar*. Where is our *Ronald Reagan*? Where is Europe's *Churchill*?

We face a crisis of moral clarity where the foundation of civilization is being cast aside as men are marrying men and women are marrying women. The Ten Commandments are ridiculed and removed as the traditional American family unravels without a moral compass and crumbles, lacking foundations that are unshakable.

The crisis of America extends to our educational system, whose graduates from secondary school can neither read nor write, thus guaranteeing a permanent underclass locked into the living hell of eternal poverty. No nation spends more on education than America, and yet our students rank in math and science on an international scale near the bottom—beneath many third-world countries. This is indeed a matter of national security. As a nation, we are now determining who we are going to be in the future. We are taking a look at where we have been and where we are right now. History has proven that when you forget the mistakes of the past, you will repeat those same mistakes in the future. How can America avoid that? What do we need to know and who do we need to be to ensure America's position as a world leader in the future?

When the Founding Fathers wrote the Declaration of Independence, they declared all Americans to be free from England. They proclaimed to the world that America was one nation under God and endowed by her Creator—God—with certain inalienable rights, including the right to life, liberty, and the pursuit of happiness.

LIFE, LIBERTY, AND THE PURSUIT OF HAPPINESS TODAY

George Washington, our first president and the "father of this nation," made these important comments: "It is impossible to rightly govern the world without God and the Bible."[1] "Do not let anyone claim to be a true American patriot if they ever attempt to separate religion from politics."[2] Abraham Lincoln said that the Bible was "the best gift God has given to man."[3]

Certainly the ACLU would disagree with those quotes today. Today, the Judeo-Christian religion is slowly being excluded from American society. There is no prayer or Bible reading in public schools. When I went to public school, we started every day with prayer and a devotional over the public address system. That's gone forever.

The Ten Commandments are now being removed from schools and from the front of government facilities because we do not want "freedom of religion." The ACLU is trying to drive "freedom from religion" down our throats. The 9th U.S. Circuit Court of Appeals in California has ruled that the phrase "one nation under God" is unconstitutional.[4]

What about the "life, liberty, and the pursuit of happiness" guaranteed to all Americans by *the Constitution*? Life is a gift from God, yet every day four thousand innocent babies in America are murdered in the wombs of their mothers through abortion.[5] Mother Teresa said, and I quote, "The nation that murders a baby in the womb of the mother has lost its soul." I quite agree. God bless Mother Teresa.

In its current debates over the sanctity of marriage, America is now considering the very principle that brought the judgment of God to Sodom and Gomorrah. If God does not judge America, He's going to have to apologize to Sodom and Gomorrah. If homosexual marriage becomes a reality, there will be no legal reason to prevent polygamy. If we step off this moral cliff, America will not recover from the fall. Peggy Noonan, author of *When Character Was King,* said, "Americans are carrying around in their heads...a sense that the wheels are coming off the trolley, and the trolley...off the tracks, and hurtling forward, toward an unknown destination."[6] She's absolutely right. America is in a moral and economic free fall.

The average time span of the world's greatest civilizations is approximately two hundred years. America is now nearly two hundred thirty-three years old. If we do not have a return to righteousness, the greatest days in America are not in front of us; they are behind us.

THE DECLINE OF AMERICA

Alexander Tyler, a Scottish historian, charted the progression of the world's greatest civilizations from their birth, to the zenith of their power, and then to their fall. This progression of civilizations includes eight critical steps. Can you identify America's rise and fall?

1. From bondage to eminent spiritual faith
2. From spiritual faith to great courage
3. From courage to liberty
4. From liberty to abundance
5. From abundance to complacency
6. From complacency to apathy
7. From apathy to dependence
8. From dependence back to bondage

In my opinion, America is now at step seven—from apathy to dependence. *Dependence* is the word that describes America. We are dependent on foreign oil to keep our economy from crashing, and 70 percent of that oil is coming from foreign countries that want to see America fall. America is no longer a *producing* nation; we have become a *consuming* nation. Our jobs have been sent to foreign countries. The words "Made in America" that used to be on the labels of clothing now read, "Made in China," "Made in Korea," "Made in Vietnam," or India, Mexico, or any other country except the United States of America.

America is swimming in debt. The trade imbalance has put billions of American dollars in the hands of the Chinese government.[7] China is now using our money to buy up American companies. You don't have to be an economic scientist to discern how negative that can be. America is *dependent* on China's goodwill not to substitute the U.S. dollar with the euro as the currency of exchange. If China ever dumped the U.S. dollar, it would cause our economy to crash, without fail.

Diana and I have traveled to Europe and the Middle East since the seventies, and until two years ago the American dollar was a welcomed currency. Recently the desired form of exchange has been the euro. The dollar is losing its influence.

Russia, China, and Iran—an axis of evil since the early nineties—are united against America and Israel. Just a few days ago, the Russians pledged to sell long-range bombers to Iran to retaliate against Israel.[8]

Iran's President Ahmadinejad has made enormous strides in 2008 toward his goal of obtaining nuclear weapons. The Atomic Energy Agency has reported that Iran now has thirty-eight hundred uranium enrichment centrifuges in full-time operation. Most of these centrifuges have been upgraded to more modern models that take much less time to enrich even more uranium than could be done previously. Some estimates predict that Iran will have enough enriched uranium for a nuclear weapon in less than one year.

In 2008 President Ahmadinejad has also continued to threaten Israel, calling for that nation to be utterly destroyed. Even as Israel celebrated its sixtieth birthday, Iran's president was declaring:

> Those who think they can revive the stinking corpse of the usurping and fake Israeli regime by throwing a birthday party are seriously mistaken. Today the reason for the Zionist regime's existence is questioned, and this regime is on its way to annihilation.[9]

While Iran made progress in its race for nuclear weapons in 2008, it was a year filled with indecision and inaction for America and the international community. Recently the United Nations Security Council failed to reach an agreement on economic sanctions against Iran. The Congress of the United States also failed to impose new economic sanctions on Iran before it left for its winter recess.[10]

As we speak, Russia has invaded Georgia, and remains there, fully intending to control the oil flowing through Georgia. Look on a world map—the road from Russia through Georgia leads straight to Israel.

AMERICA'S ROLE IN THE FUTURE

What is America's role in the end-of-the-age prophecy? The truthful answer is that America has no significant role because no specific mention of the United States can be found in the Bible. Russia and its allies are going into Israel "to take plunder and to take booty." Russia is going to move militarily against Israel from the north to seize the great mineral wealth and natural resources that are there. They will promise the Islamic nations control of Jerusalem and the Temple Mount. What will be America's response to this brazen act of invading and raping Israel of its wealth? Ezekiel 38:13 gives the answer:

> Sheba, Dedan, the merchants of Tarshish, and all their young lions will say to you, "Have you come to take plunder? Have you gathered your army to take booty, to carry away silver and gold, to take away livestock and goods, to take great plunder?"

"Sheba, Dedan, the merchants of Tarshish [that is, the Western powers] and all their young lions," will be upset when Russia invades Israel. (England's symbol is that of a lion.) America is an offspring of England, hence "the young lions" will not come to Israel's rescue. They will not send massive military forces to drive Russia and the Arabs out of Israel. Instead, the Western world is simply going to make a passive diplomatic response, saying, "Have you gathered your army to take booty, to carry away silver and gold, to take away livestock and goods, to take great plunder?"

What a ridiculous response!

It's obvious to the nations of the world what Russia and the Arabs are doing, and yet the Western world is doing absolutely nothing to stop them. Why won't America respond? Let me venture to say that after America's extended war in Iraq, the next administration will probably withdraw from Iraq, vowing to stay out of the Middle East in the future.

America's great debt leads to military weakness. As voices in Congress cry out for us to withdraw from Iraq, they will certainly refrain from starting a shooting war with Russia in the Middle East.

When America sees Russia and the Arabs going into Israel, it will be simply a war above and beyond its national will to respond. Russia and the Arab nations will form one of the most impressive military forces ever put together. As Ezekiel says, "It will cover the land" (Ezek. 38:16).

Ezekiel makes it clear that America's and Europe's diplomatic inquiry means absolutely nothing to Russia and the Arabs. The invasion is on! This invasion is described as follows:

> You will come up against My people Israel like a cloud, to cover the land. It will be in the latter days that *I will bring you against My land*, so that the nations may know Me, when I am hallowed in you, O Gog, before their eyes.
> —EZEKIEL 38:16, EMPHASIS ADDED

God makes it clear that He is dragging Russia and its allies into Israel: "I will bring you against My land." When Russia leads its Arab allies into Israel, the Western superpowers simply watch.

I believe that after years of repeated acts of violent terrorism on Israel and the world by Islamic fanatics, the Western nations have become gun-shy about attacking a Russian-Arab military alliance.

Since September 11, 2001, terrorist attacks on Israel and other nations have dramatically increased. In 2002 there were 85 recorded acts of terrorism in the world with more than half occurring in Israel. The current acts of recorded terrorism as of this writing is 184, doubling the total recorded in 2007. Only 10 of the 184 murderous acts occurred in Israel.[11]

Terrorism is spreading rapidly around the world while the West sleeps, but the God who protects Israel "neither slumbers nor sleeps" (Ps. 121:3).

THE FINAL FOUR

The Bible is very clear that the major players on the stage of world prophecy at the "end of the age" will be:

- The king of the North: Russia
- The king of the South: Islamic nations
- The king of the East: China
- The king of the West: Europe, led by the Antichrist (Ezekiel 37)

The next major prophetic event that's going to happen in prophecy is the Rapture of the church. For those who do not understand the Rapture of the church, it's described very clearly in 1 Corinthians 15:51–58. Paul says, "In a moment, in the twinkling of an eye, at the last trump: for the trumpet shall sound, and the dead shall be raised incorruptible, and we shall be changed" (v. 52, KJV).

In Revelation 19:9 we read, "Blessed are those who are called to the marriage supper of the Lamb!" The marriage supper takes place in heaven. Christians will be called to heaven in the Rapture.

Some people have a hard time understanding the Rapture of the church. You may be one of them and may be thinking, "Nothing like that has ever happened!" But it has! In the Old Testament, Elijah was taken into heaven in a chariot of fire (2 Kings 2:11). He is in heaven, and he has not died; he will die, but he hasn't yet. The Bible says, "And as it is appointed for men to die once, but after this the judgment" (Heb. 9:27). Elijah is going to be killed on the streets of Jerusalem as one of the two witnesses mentioned in Revelation (Rev. 11:7).

Both Enoch and Jesus were taken into heaven; so don't say

people can't be snatched off the earth and transported to heaven. It's a clear and historical biblical fact that has happened. These people were taken alive from the earth into heaven, and they have been there for centuries.

What would happen if millions of Christians left the earth in the twinkling of an eye? The majority of those left on Earth are committed to the prince of darkness and the Antichrist (Rev. 8:12). Remember that the church is the light of the world (Matt. 5:14), and when the light of the world is gone, darkness rules. That's why Satan is called *the prince of darkness* (Eph. 6:12).

What does that mean? The word *prince* means "a position of authority." The word *darkness* indicates a condition. When the world becomes totally spiritually dark, Satan will have absolute control.

What will happen then? Ten world leaders are going to come out of Europe and consolidate the Western world under their absolute authority. This coalition of ten leaders under the leadership of the Antichrist will rule with an iron fist to stop the global financial chaos created by the exodus of millions of Christians from the world's workforce.

Financial weakness and military weakness go hand in hand. America's present enormous national debt and the anticipated growth of that debt will weaken her ability to make a military response against any threat in the free world.

THE RISE OF THE ANTICHRIST

From among the ten leaders will arise the Antichrist prophesied about in Daniel 9:26. He is going to come as a man of peace. He will conquer three of the ten leaders and will become the new *Caesar* of Western civilization.

The Antichrist will force every person on Earth to take his mark on his or her forehead or hand. Without this mark, no one can buy or sell even a pair of shoelaces.

The method I believe the Antichrist will use to conquer the other leaders and nations will be by creating peace treaties! In Daniel 7, Daniel says that this Antichrist will get the attention of people by the "sound of the great words" he speaks (Dan.

7:11, AMP). Other translations describe his words as "boastful" and "arrogant." I believe that means he is going to make peace treaties he never intends to keep, much like the principle of *hudna* observed by radical Islam.

Although in many cases today's media have described *hudna* as a "legitimate and binding contract," in reality *hudna* refers to a peace treaty made but never intended to be kept, because it is only advancing your cause to conquer your enemy.[12]

The Antichrist is a false messiah. He is going to make a seven-year peace treaty with Israel, prophesied in Daniel 9:27. Exactly 2,520 days after that treaty is signed, Jesus Christ is going to return to the earth at Jerusalem. This is the Second Coming. Do not confuse the Rapture, which is going to happen any day, with the Second Coming. The Second Coming occurs seven prophetic years after that peace treaty is signed.

We can be sure about the exact number of days because the Bible is a mathematical text. A prophetic year is exactly 360 days. Seven times 360 is 2,520. And the Bible clearly says that at the end of seven years, the Lord Jesus Christ is returning to set up His kingdom in the city of Jerusalem.

The Antichrist is going to break the seven-year treaty with Israel after three and a half years, or forty-two months. He will set up his image, where he is to be worshiped, and he will establish a one-world government.

Today we can see the beginnings of that one-world government by what is currently happening within the United Nations. In my opinion, the United Nations is *a united nothing*. They are corrupt and couldn't settle a fight between two Boy Scouts in the backyard. But they are the beginning of a one-world government.

After the Antichrist establishes his one-world government, he will establish a one-world religion. That religion is now coming to the earth in the form of secular humanism. Humanism will accept any god but the God of Abraham, Isaac, and Jacob.

The Antichrist will also create a one-world currency and an economic system so air-tight that no one on earth can buy or sell anything without his permission or knowledge. Revelation 13:16–18 (KJV) reads:

And he [the Antichrist] causeth all, both small and great, rich and poor, free and bond, to receive a mark in their right hand, or in their foreheads: and that no man might buy or sell, save he that had the mark, or the name of the beast [Antichrist], or the number of his name....And his number is Six hundred threescore and six.

The technology already exists via computer and high-tech chips inserted under the skin to fulfill John the Revelator's prediction some two thousand years ago from the Isle of Patmos.

Revelation 13 declares that the Antichrist will be the head of the European Union. This charismatic political wonder will do the following things, recorded in his full résumé, which is given by Daniel in chapter 8:

This false messiah and chief son of Satan will:

1. *Have supernatural demonic power to know the unknown.* The Bible says he will have a "fierce countenance, and understanding dark sentences" (KJV), or "understands sinister schemes" (Dan. 8:23, NKJV). It will not be possible to keep anything a secret from him because of this satanic power.

2. *"Cause craft to prosper"* (v. 25, KJV). Hitler came to power in Germany because the economy of Germany was in chaos. He rebuilt the economy of Germany, bringing prosperity and pride to a nation that had been crushed by the Peace Treaty of Versailles in 1919. As Germany's "messiah," he became a monster, sweeping the world into the Holocaust and bringing twelve years of living hell to the earth.

   The coming Antichrist will come to power at a time of international economic crisis. He will cause craft and global industry to prosper. No man will be able to buy or sell anything without having the mark of the beast on his right hand or forehead. (See Revelation 13:17.) This Antichrist will control the world's economy with a vengeance.

The economy of the world will flourish. Then, like Hitler, he will drag the world into the Battle of Armageddon, a literal bloodbath the equal of which the world has never seen.

3. *Make a seven-year peace treaty with Israel, which he will break at the end of three and a half years.* He "...by peace shall destroy many" (Dan. 8:25, KJV). He will be shot in the head and miraculously recover, emulating the death and resurrection of Jesus Christ. At this point, he will turn on the Jewish people. Daniel writes that he "shall destroy the mighty and the holy people" (v. 24, KJV).

The "holy people" are the Jews. They are the authors of the Word of God. They produced the patriarchs and the prophets. They are the source of knowledge about Jesus Christ and the twelve disciples. Without the Jewish contribution to Christianity there would be no Christianity.

When the Antichrist begins to attack the Jewish people, they will flee to Petra in Jordan, where they will be supernaturally protected by God Himself from this monster.

4. *Be a prideful powermonger.* This false messiah "shall exalt [magnify] himself in his heart" (Dan. 8:25). Revelation 13:5 confirms this by saying: "He was given a mouth speaking great things and blasphemies, and he was given authority to continue for forty-two months," or three and a half years. This demonic world leader will create a one-world government, a one-world currency, and a one-world religion. One need only be a casual observer of current events to see that all three of these things are coming into reality.

5. *Oppose Jesus Christ Himself.* "He shall even rise against the Prince of princes" (Dan. 8:25). At the Battle of Armageddon, this chief son of Satan, this

false messiah with enormous demonic power, will oppose Jesus Christ Himself. However, he will not be successful! He will be bound and cast into the bottomless pit by the Conqueror from Calvary.

THE END-OF-THE-AGE EVENTS RECORDED IN REVELATION

The Book of Revelation describes the end of the age through the symbolism of seven seals, seven trumpets, and seven vials. (See Revelation 6–8, 16.) These images represent the twenty-one specific judgments that God is going to bring to the earth. During these punishments, one-third of the earth's population will perish. The Battle of Armageddon follows the pouring of the sixth vial (Rev. 16:12–16).

The four horsemen of the apocalypse

Revelation speaks about four riders on horses, who have become known as *the four horsemen of the apocalypse*. (See Revelation 6:2; 9:17.) The first horseman to appear is riding a white horse. This rider symbolizes deceit, false prophets, and false teachers, and is known as the Antichrist. He comes with a bow with no arrows (representing war and deceit). He also comes with one crown (representing the prince of darkness of this world, who wears a crown). "And I looked, and behold, a white horse. He who sat on it had a bow; and a crown was given to him, and he went out conquering and to conquer" (Rev. 6:2).

He must not be confused with Jesus Christ who comes riding on a white horse in Revelation 19, wearing many crowns (symbolizing the King of kings) and a sword coming from His mouth (representing the Word of God).

The second rider sits on the red horse and carries a great sword. He symbolizes war and the blood spilled in battle as men kill each other. "Another horse, fiery red, went out. And it was granted to the one who sat on it to take peace from the earth, and that people should kill one another; and there was given to him a great sword" (Rev. 6:4).

The third rider sits on the black horse and is called *Famine*. He carries a balance in his hand (representing drought and global starvation). "When He opened the third seal, I heard the third living creature say, 'Come and see.' So I looked, and behold, a black horse, and he who sat on it had a pair of scales in his hand. And I heard a voice in the midst of the four living creatures saying, 'A quart of wheat for a denarius, and three quarts of barley for a denarius; and do not harm the oil and the wine'" (Rev. 6:5–6).

The final and fourth horse is the pale horse, which is named *Death*. "So I looked, and behold, a pale horse. And the name of him who sat on it was Death, and Hades followed with him. And power was given to them over a fourth of the earth, to kill with sword, with hunger, with death, and by the beasts of the earth" (Rev. 6:8).

These four horsemen are the forces of destruction described in the Book of Revelation. They are referred to by the dangers they represent: conquest, war, famine, and death.

In stark contrast, Revelation 19 describes a white horse who ushers in He who is "called Faithful and True...and The Word of God." His eyes are "like a flame of fire," and He wears "many crowns." On His robe and thigh is written "King of kings and Lord of lords" (Rev. 19:11–16)! Jesus Christ is coming back to rule and reign in the city of Jerusalem for one thousand years of perfect peace. It will be the Golden Age, when the lion shall lie down with the lamb, when men shall beat their swords into plowshares and study war no more.

The first time Jesus came, He came as a baby in Bethlehem's manger; the next time He comes, He is coming as King of kings! The first time He came riding on a mule; the next time He comes, He is riding on a milk-white stallion followed by the armies in heaven, including the bride of Christ.

Christ's return will bring with it the binding of Satan: "Then I saw an angel coming down from heaven, having the key to the bottomless pit and a great chain in his hand. He laid hold of the dragon, that serpent of old, who is the Devil and Satan, and bound him for a thousand years; and he cast him into the bottomless pit, and shut him up, and set a seal on him, so that he should deceive the nations no more till the thousand years were finished. But after these things he must be released for a little while" (Rev. 20:1–3).

RUSSIA LEADS THE ATTACK AGAINST ISRAEL

Some time after the Rapture of the church, Russia will lead Iran and the Islamic nations of the world in an attack against Israel, as described in Ezekiel 38.

> I will turn you around, put hooks into your jaws, and lead you out, with all your army, horses, and horsemen, all splendidly clothed, a great company with bucklers and shields, all of them handling swords. Persia, Ethiopia, and Libya are with them, all of them with shield and helmet.
> —EZEKIEL 38:4–5

Why will Russia come to Israel? Let's take a look at some of the reasons for Russia's interest in conquering Israel.

1. Russia will come to Israel because they need a warm-water entrance into the oceans of the world. The Middle East offers that. Russia, under Putin's leadership, earlier made a multibillion-dollar oil contract with Saddam Hussein, and today Russia has begun a determined campaign to preserve the sanctity of all the contracts signed by its oil, gas, and affiliated construction companies for oil investment projects in Iraq. In addition, increasingly, Iran is recognized by Moscow as another strategic energy partner for Russia.[13] Russia has also allowed their scientists to direct Iran's nuclear weapons programs to destroy Israel. Putin is the former director of the KGB who has removed the democratic process from Russia and, at the same time, charmed the West into neutrality.

2. Russia must have access to an unlimited supply of oil to regain the stature of a global superpower. For years, Russia has been building its relationships with oil-producing Islamic nations.

The trade-off between Russia and the Islamic nations is exposed by the prophet Ezekiel, who wrote concerning a Russian-Islamic alliance, saying, "Be thou prepared, and prepare for thyself [speaking of Russia], thou, and all thy company that are assembled unto thee [Islamic alliance], and be thou a guard unto them" (Ezek. 38:7, KJV). "Be thou a guard unto them" more accurately translates, "Be a leader over them or a captain unto them."

Thousands of years ago, Ezekiel saw the Russian-Islamic alliance, identified the nations, identified their target (Israel), and clearly stated that Russia would be the leader of the pack. Today you can often see it on the evening news.

3. The mineral deposits in the Dead Sea are so great they can't be properly appraised on today's market. It is estimated that the Dead Sea contains two billion tons of potassium chloride, which is potash needed to enrich the soil that is rapidly being depleted around the world. The Dead Sea also contains twenty-two billion tons of magnesium chloride and twelve billion tons of sodium chloride.[14] The wealth of the Dead Sea has the Russian bear salivating at the mouth.

Through Ezekiel, God said to Russia, "I will put hooks in your jaws." God is going to drag Russia into Israel. Why? Throughout its history, Russia has been anti-Semitic and, in its final form, will be led by a dictator who will lead an Arab coalition of nations to crush Israel. God makes it clear that He will judge Russia in the land of Israel, and Russia, with its Islamic alliance, will be annihilated (Ezek. 39:2, KJV).

ARMAGEDDON

John the Revelator describes the mother of all wars—the final battle on Earth at Armageddon.

> And I saw coming out of the mouth of the dragon [Satan] and out of the mouth of the beast [the Antichrist] and out of the mouth of the false prophet [the religious leader of the Antichrist], three unclean spirits like frogs; for they are spirits of demons, performing signs, which go out to the kings of the whole world, to gather them together for a war of the great day of God, the Almighty....And they gathered them together to the place Hebrew called Har-Magedon.
>
> —REVELATION 16:13–14, 16, NAS

This passage says that the satanic trinity consisting of Satan, his chief son the Antichrist, and the demonized spiritual leader called the false prophet are calling the nations of the world to war.

Russia and the Islamic Alliance were annihilated about three and a half years previously in Israel by the hand of God. Now comes the final battle for the supremacy of Planet Earth—the Battle of Armageddon.

It's the king of the East, China, against the king of the West. The West will be led by the Antichrist. China will be coming to this battlefield walking down the dry bed of the River Euphrates with an army of two hundred million men. Think of it!

The Bible says the blood on this battlefield will flow to the bridle of a horse for a distance of two hundred miles. It staggers the mind to comprehend this sea of human blood.

As you read earlier, the hook in the jaw of both these armies is their desperate need for oil. Both must have it for their armies to be victorious and for their national economies to thrive. It is perfectly clear in this prophetic drama that America is no longer a superpower. America is no longer the world's policeman, as we have been since World War I.

FIVE EVENTS AFFECTING AMERICA

There are five events that eliminate America as a superpower.

1. The election of a president who has a "retreat in defeat" foreign policy

The first event would be the election of a president who has a "retreat in defeat" foreign policy. For this to happen, a majority of Americans would have to grow so tired of fighting foreign wars that they would support an isolationist or appeasement mentality. They would do nothing to defend Israel or any other country. We have just elected a new leadership with a party shift in Congress. We will soon know whether our new leaders are going to defend democracy or retreat in defeat.

2. A terrorist attack

President Ahmadinejad has already promised to share Iran's nuclear weapons with all terrorist organizations. It would be simple to smuggle several dirty bombs across the Mexican or Canadian borders into America in backpacks.

A dirty bomb small enough to be carried in a backpack could easily kill one million Americans per bomb. The government has revealed that it believes terrorists plan to attack several cities at one time, using backpack or suitcase bombs.[15]

If terrorists smuggled in bombs using backpacks or suitcases, attacking seven or eight American cities simultaneously, millions of Americans would lie dead in the streets of our major cities. Our borders are wide open. It could happen. That's why it is imperative that our country establish control of the borders between America, Mexico, and Canada.

3. The Rapture of millions of Christians

The third reason America will not be a significant prophetic superpower in the future is the Rapture of millions of Christians. According to church attendance, America has more Christians per capita than any other nation on earth.[16] If the Rapture happened today and millions of Christians were suddenly gone, every sector of our society would suffer a staggering blow, including the U.S. economy, government, and military.

When Christians are raptured out of America, America will immediately stop the majority of her support of Israel. When the church in America is gone and America rejects Israel, the judgment of God will fall upon America.

Take note of this: the time is short! Everything is coming to a head so aggressively and so rapidly that all the players of prophecy, as prophesied by Ezekiel, are now on the stage of world history for the first time. Israel has been reborn. And the major nations represented in Bible prophecy are poised and ready for the next step. China and Iran are both becoming major players. Europe is rebirthing the Roman Empire. Radical Islam is threatening the world. Russia has invaded Georgia, demonstrating that it wants to be a world superpower again. All of these nations want world domination!

As these major players at the end of this prophetic age prepare to make their aggressive moves toward world dominance, each nation must have one thing to keep its economy afloat and its military forces fighting. *That one thing is oil.*

In a few years, the energy crisis we are currently facing in America can be solved. It can be solved with electric cars, wind and solar energy, alternative fuels, and atomic energy. Who needs oil? We do, and we need it right now! All nations need it right now.

That's why a window of opportunity exists *now* for radical Islam and anti-American foreign powers (example, Russia and Venezuela) to use what it has—*oil*—to bring America and the world to their knees. If there was ever a time for you to stand up for America, to stand up for democracy, to stand up for freedom, it's right now!

Are you ready for the Rapture of the church? Get ready! It's going to happen, and it's going to happen very soon.

4. The oil crisis ushers in a U.S. economic crash

The fourth event that prevents America from being a prophetic superpower is the reality of an oil crisis that will ultimately bring the United States to an economic crash.

The 1979 oil crisis during the Carter administration illustrates the potential for this to happen. OPEC told America to stop its support of Israel or suffer the consequences. America stood by Israel, and OPEC slowed down our oil imports, causing our economy to experience 19–20 percent inflation.

Think about it. In 1979 we were only importing 25 percent of our oil. Now it's about 70 percent. Make no mistake; we are far more vulnerable right now than we were during the Carter administration. OPEC is still controlled by nations that hate Israel and the Jewish people. If OPEC decides to slow down or stop oil imports to America, our economy would come to a screeching halt. We certainly could not remain a military superpower for very long.

It is imperative that America finds alternative sources of energy—and does so immediately! It is a matter of national security. It is a must for our very survival!

The time clock leading to the fulfillment of Bible prophecy concerning the "end of the age" is ticking away. We cannot stop these prophetic events from taking place. The events are on God's timetable, not ours. They will usher in the return of Christ to establish His kingdom forever. Just as you can make certain that you are ready to be a part of the great Rapture of the church when we will be transported to our heavenly home for eternity, so too you can make certain that you are living on Earth until that time with the blessings of God upon your home, your family, and your finances.

5. An economic crash, leading to the death of the dollar

In the last chapter I discussed "America's Economic Meltdown: The Perfect Storm." The elements of the "perfect storm" are represented by the subprime lending crisis, America's addiction to foreign oil, making it possible for us to be controlled by nations who want to see us destroyed, major bank failures, and China's bank filled with 1.5 trillion U.S. dollars received via the trade imbalance. China has the financial power right now to join with nations hostile to America and dump the U.S. dollar as the currency by which all debts, both foreign and domestic, are paid. They could dump the dollar for the euro, and the U.S. dollar would collapse. Be certain that the crises on Wall Street are not over by any means.

Chapter 4

A FIGHT FOR WORLD CONTROL

IRAN IS RACING TOWARD NUCLEAR WEAPONS AND PROMISES to wipe Israel off the map. President Ahmadinejad has made it clear that he also intends to attack America. One of the ultimate weapons of war is oil. America is facing an oil crisis that affects every person in our nation and threatens our national security.

The recent Iranian missile test presented yet another round of intense speculation that war might erupt between Iran, Israel, and the United States. Let's get our facts straight. Iran has been in conflict with Israel and America since 1979 as it came to power under the present theocratic dictatorship.

The crisis facing America and Israel is the reality of weapons that are now available to Iran for use against both countries. Radical Islamic Iranians refer to America as "the Great Satan," and Israel as the "little Satan," and are no longer content with simple truck bombs and suicide bombers wearing vests laden with explosives.

With the help of Russia, China, and North Korea, Iran has produced an array of antiship missiles, mines, and speedboats capable of sinking vessels in the Strait of Hormuz.[1] Now they are trying to put together monster weapons—nuclear missiles and bombs.

THE THREAT OF IRAN

In a matter of months, Iran is going to be in position to execute the threats of President Ahmadinejad to "wipe Israel off the map."[2] In a television interview in June 2008, Ahmadinejad said, "Today, the time for the fall of the satanic power of the United States has come and the countdown to the annihilation of the emperor of power and wealth has started."[3] President Ahmadinejad has made his intentions very clear.

America, it's time for us to wake up! Many Americans look at our Star Wars military defense system and assume a false sense of security. Let me remind you that on 9/11 more than three thousand Americans were murdered in cold blood in the twin towers of the World Trade Center in New York City, the Pentagon, and a field in Pennsylvania. How were they murdered? Not by nations with guided missiles...not by high-tech weaponry...not by divisions of an invading army...but by eighteen radical Islamic fanatics with box cutters who used our hijacked airliners as missiles of death to kill our own people. That was not sophisticated. It was caveman technology, but it proved to be very successful.

September 11 proved that radical Islam has the will to kill Americans, and they have the will to conquer us. They just lack the power. But Iran is racing toward the development of nuclear weapons. They're working day and night. They're ignoring every form of diplomacy. They are ignoring the mandates of the Atomic Energy Commission.

When they have that nuclear weapon, radical Islam will have the power—and will use it to attack *you* and *your family*. We face a real danger. We, the United States of America, have an enemy that intends to destroy us. We need to come out of political correctness and come to the world of reality. Americans will slip from stage seven to eight, "dependence back into bondage," if we allow nuclear weapons to get in the hands of our enemies.

President Ahmadinejad believes that if he starts World War III, the Islamic messiah will suddenly and mysteriously appear. Understand that he doesn't know *who* this messiah is or *where* he is, but he believes the moment that Iran starts this "holy war," which will engulf the entire world, his messiah will appear. He will lead the "holy warriors" of radical Islam to a global *Sharia*, meaning that every nation on the face of the earth will be under Islamic law. Ahmadinejad believes that he has the power and the duty to bring this about.

Remember, history teaches us that those who fail to remember the mistakes of the past are doomed to repeat them in the future. One of the most tragic events of recent history was Hitler's Holocaust against the Jewish people during World War II. There are a number of lessons that we can learn from the Holocaust, but one of the most important is this: when a maniac threatens to kill you, take him at his maniacal word.

When Hitler began his threats to kill the Jewish people, few took him seriously. That was a tragic mistake. Ahmadinejad is the *new Hitler of the Middle East*. He wants a nuclear holocaust. He wants "the Great Satan," which is America, to fall and be in submission to Islam, and he wants to utterly destroy Israel.

Several years ago, former prime minister of Israel Benjamin Netanyahu sat in my office and told me that when he was in office, he gave photographic proof to America's intelligence community that Russia was helping Iran develop missiles capable of hitting Jerusalem, London, and New York. Our intelligence agencies did not believe his information until he gave them pictorial proof that it was happening.

That was years ago. Now on national television, you see Iran shooting missiles to demonstrate to the world that they have the technology.

When Iran obtains nuclear ability—and they will unless they are stopped by a preemptive military strike—they will be able to put nuclear warheads on those missiles. Can you imagine the global chaos that would be created if New York, London, and Jerusalem were all hit with nuclear missiles at the same time?

There are many Americans who do not believe that Iran can launch a nuclear weapon that will land in America. They are absolutely wrong! In recent testimony before the House Armed Services Committee (HASC), Dr. William Graham, chairman of the Commission to Assess the Threat to the United States from Electromagnetic Pulse (EMP) Attack, a blue-ribbon panel established by Congress in 2001, warned that the U.S. intelligence community "doesn't have a story" to explain the recent Iranian nuclear tests. In his testimony, he stated:

> The only plausible explanation we can find is that the Iranians are figuring out how to launch a missile from a ship and get it up to altitude and then detonate it. And that's exactly what you would do if you had a nuclear weapon on a Scud or a Shahab-3 or other missile, and you wanted to explode it over the United States.[4]

By launching a nuclear missile off a ship, Iran could make good on their pledge to bring about "a world without America." They don't need to have the ability to launch the missile across the ocean. But they can bring a ship within a hundred miles of America's coastline and launch their missiles from there.

In *Jerusalem Countdown,* I wrote about the EMP, an electromagnetic pulse device that could totally stop all forms of electricity.[5] During his testimony before the HASC, Dr. Graham warned that Iran has the ability to execute such an attack on America, which would wipe out all electrical capability in America.[6]

Simply stated, a missile carrying enriched plutonium would explode in the atmosphere over the United States of America. Within a matter of seconds, all electrical power would be disabled. Radio and television stations would go off the air. Telephones would not work. Cars, trucks, tractors—all motor vehicles—would not start. The refrigerators and freezers in your home would fail to function, and all your food would spoil. The Internet—today's techno-communications superstar, would be inaccessible.

Think about this: The president of the United States would not be able to communicate with military leaders around the world. All communication of any kind would grind to a halt! We would be back in the days of the pony express! Iran has the power to do this. It's not as difficult as you may think.

FOUR CRITICAL STEPS TO STOP IRAN

America is in a war for its survival. Many Americans do not want to admit it, but that is the truth. Executing an extensive preemptive military strike against Iran will most certainly lead to a world conflict. Once the nuclear genie gets out of the bottle in the Middle East, there will be no stopping World War III. There are four ways the American people can stop what is happening in the Middle East without firing a shot.

1. Americans can divest their stocks from private and public pension portfolios that are attached to Iran.

Every state in the United States has pension funds filled with assets worth billions of dollars. Many Americans have invested a portion of their wages into pension funds that in turn invest in overseas stocks and private equity stocks. In a Reuters report dated January 16, 2008, we can see that the United States has invested more than $3.6 billion dollars in Iran's petrochemical, gas, and oil industries.[7]

If you—and every other American—would remove stocks and investments from Iran-owned industries and ask your governor and state legislators to divest public funds from Iran, the billions of U.S. dollars that they're currently using to make weapons would be removed from their economy.

The state of Florida was one of the first states to pass divestment legislation. The state of Texas has already begun to divest. Several bills have recently been put before Congress that would restrict U.S. cooperation with states and companies doing business with Iran. Legislative proposals have also been put forth that would order pension funds to divest from firms with commercial links to Iran.[8] But with the onset of our most recent economic crisis, there is some indication that the push for divestment may be changing. A recent report by Craig Karmin, a reporter for the "Money and Investing" section of the *Wall Street Journal*, states:

> Recently, with markets pummeling most pension funds, this hard-line stance is coming under greater scrutiny. Lawmakers are opting for less-stringent bills, offering

fund managers more flexibility or simply rejecting new divestment measures.[9]

Americans must continue to see the critical need to demand that America stop financing Iran's nuclear power advancements.

Why are OPEC leaders holding emergency meetings regarding the price of oil? Because their income is presently falling like a rock.

Iran is experiencing a rapid decrease in income with the current economic global meltdown. Our enemies don't want us to find alternative energy sources. They don't want us to conserve energy, and they certainly don't want us drilling for oil. They want to hold us hostage to their oil so we can finance their nuclear productions and maniacal dreams of a nuclear holocaust for Israel.

If the mere mention of conservation, alternative fuel sources, and added drilling causes OPEC leaders to suddenly assemble, what would happen if we divested our dollars, drilled for oil on our own soil, developed alternative fuel sources, and conserved our energy?

We could stop the flow of seventy billion dollars per year to countries that seek our destruction.

The energy crisis is the "Achilles' heel" of America's security. We *must* solve this energy crisis, and solve it *now*!

2. Drill here; drill now. Drill, baby, drill!

The second step we can take is to call our U.S. senator or congressman and tell them to start drilling for oil right now in the United States of America. Drill in Anwar. Drill offshore. Drill in Colorado. Drill in Wyoming. Drill in Utah. Drill in your bathtub if there is a chance you might strike oil.

America must end its addiction to foreign oil. We need to develop wind power, nuclear power, bio power, solar power, coal power, and every alternative fuel source imaginable. Every person in America needs to get that message in his or her mind. We should make our position against foreign oil dependence clear by voting against every person in Congress who is preventing alternative fuel development from happening.

We are a democracy—and government officials are elected

to work for the people. We can vote them in, and we can vote them out.

I would suggest that you take a look at the voting records of your state and government officials, and if they have voted against any form of drilling...vote them out of office. You can do that to help save America. Breaking our addiction to foreign oil is a matter of national security.

3. Develop effective antimissile defenses.

Russia vigorously objects to the NATO antimissile system. But with their recent invasion of Georgia, they have demonstrated their intention to lead a military armada that will attempt to make Russia a superpower once again. And believe me, Russia is in Georgia because they want their oil. They want to control that seaport.

Russia has been in bed with Iran and China since 1990, and I believe they have demonstrated that they care nothing about America's future. Israel has developed an antimissile defense system, and so should America.

4. Help the Iranian people liberate themselves from the country's theocratic dictators.

I know of Iranians—who call themselves *Persians*—who visit Iran annually to be with their family members. They report that 70 percent of Iranians want to be liberated from the religious fanatics who are controlling their country. Think about that. At least 70 percent want to be liberated, but they are being controlled by the radical 30 percent who have the guns.

America needs to develop and deploy an intensive and comprehensive effort to assist the Iranian people in liberating themselves. We can provide information technologies. We can send assistance to students in universities, assistance to teachers, and assistance to trade unions. In addition to these strategies, I believe that covert operations should be in play to help the Iranians liberate themselves from theocratic dictatorship.

These measures could bring dramatic results that would be far better than Iranian nuclear missiles that hit New York, Washington DC, San Francisco, Los Angeles, or any American city. I assure you that any city within one hundred miles of the coast of America is an open target for a missile launched at sea by Iran.

OIL—THE WEAPON OF WAR

We are now experiencing an economic war against America through oil. America has not built a refinery since 1976. We have been financially raped by OPEC while Congress is looking the other way. Every time you stop for gas, you experience the pain at the pump. We have enough oil offshore and in America to give us deliverance from OPEC control, yet our Congress is allowing Saudi Arabia to control our economy, our national security, and your personal financial security by bowing to OPEC's demand that we stop drilling for oil here in America.

Gas rose to more than four dollars a gallon in some states. I can remember when I bought gasoline for fifteen cents a gallon. What do you think will happen when Iran decides to stop a ship in the Strait of Hormuz, and the price of gasoline doubles to eight dollars per gallon—if you can get it at all?[10]

Several years ago on one of my television broadcasts, I said that gas would cost three dollars a gallon. People wrote me from all over the country saying, "That's impossible.... It will never happen." Now we pray for three dollars a gallon of gas!

It is a fact that the OPEC oil barons of the Middle East control America's economy and your financial security. The only way to get out of their control is by accessing the resources that America has—and using them.

With gasoline at four dollars per gallon, the average family in America will spend four thousand dollars more per year for gas. A Zogby Poll posted June 20, 2008, has shown that 74 percent of Americans favor increased offshore drilling for oil in America.[11] In spite of that, a majority of the Congress has resisted every effort to drill for more oil.

The issue of offshore drilling has been a heated discussion in our current political election-year climate. Recently, after months spent vowing to protect the nation's coastlines from new offshore oil drilling, Congress caved to the White House over the thorny issue, saying they will allow a twenty-six-year-old ban on new exploration to expire.[12]

It is my opinion, as well as that of at least 74 percent of Americans, that we need to immediately reduce the OPEC control problem. Because Americans are talking about drilling and the current economic crisis, the price of oil has begun falling and is continuing to go down as I'm writing this book. But don't forget the "price roller coaster" we have been on! Prices will go down and up again as the OPEC powers yank our puppet strings.

The current oil energy crisis has produced a new crime wave in America. Thieves are now stealing gas and diesel fuel from farms and ranches in rural areas and from gas stations. The other night while I was watching our local news, I saw one of the slickest thefts I've seen in a long time. Someone had pulled a huge trailer into a service station. From inside that trailer, thieves pulled up the floor, undid the lids to the gas tanks that were in the ground, put down huge hoses, and sucked out thousands of gallons of gas and diesel, then drove off.

Farmers are being pushed to the financial edge because people are stealing their fuel. One farmer in California made this statement: "It's an epidemic, gigantic problem. In Kern County alone, we're getting reports of five to seven diesel thefts from farms a week. It's happening in other parts of the San Joaquin Valley, too."[13]

If you enjoy eating, you need to be concerned about the well-being of agriculture in America. But it's not just happening in the farmlands of America; thieves are stealing grease from restaurants to make biofuel. Policemen are now being put on bicycles in major cities to save fuel, and others are now walking the beat instead of driving in squad cars. Think about this: it is hard to give "hot pursuit" to thieves who are stealing thousands of gallons of diesel fuel at local gas stations when you are pursuing on a bicycle!

Adding more problems to an already critical energy crisis, there has even been talk of gas rationing due to the devastating Hurricanes Gustav and Ike in 2008. Recently, John Hofmeister, former president of Shell Oil Co. and one of the most influential voices in the oil industry, called for "short-term gasoline rationing by introducing odd-even purchases based on an automobile's license plate and by limiting the amount of gasoline drivers can purchase."[14]

WHAT IS BEHIND THE ENERGY CRISIS?

During the energy crisis of 1973 we had long gas lines. Inflation rose by 20 percent. During the Carter administration, America faced one of its toughest energy crises in 1979 when OPEC instituted a series of oil price increases that sent gasoline prices skyrocketing and led to severe shortages. Why did OPEC create this gas crisis in America? The Islamic OPEC countries hate Israel, and they hate America for helping Israel. When America would not distance itself from Israel, OPEC immediately slowed down the oil production and slowed down the delivery, resulting in skyrocketing gas prices and inflation.

It can happen again! Today, 30 percent of the corn crop is going into biofuel.[15] What's the result? High food prices. Every corn product is skyrocketing. The prices of beef, chicken, and pork are also going up, because cows, chickens, and pigs eat corn! Using a food source to make a biofuel is not a bright idea.

Arab oil barons control the production of oil and have the power to blackmail the nations of the world to do their bidding. OPEC is trying to destabilize America's economy through oil. And they're trying to create hyperinflation. Unless our country starts developing a way to end the addiction to foreign oil, OPEC will be successful in its attempts to completely destroy our economy.

OPEC is also using the billions of dollars we are sending them for oil to brainwash our college and university students to hate America and Israel. In an article posted on Front PageMagazine.com, Lee Kaplan stated:

> The money the Saudis are pouring into our universities in the form of gifts and endowments is alarming: King Fahd donated $20 million dollars to set up a Middle East Studies Center at the University of Arkansas; $5 million

was donated to UC–Berkeley's Center For Middle East Studies from two Saudi sheiks linked to funding al-Qaeda; $2.5 million dollars to Harvard; $8.1 million dollars to Georgetown; $11 million dollars to Cornell; $1.5 million dollars to Texas A&M; $5 million dollars to MIT; $1 million dollars to Princeton. Rutgers received $5 million dollars to endow a chair. So did Columbia, which tried to obscure the money's source. Other recipients of Saudi largesse include UC–Santa Barbara, Johns Hopkins, Rice University, American University, University of Chicago, Syracuse University, USC, UCLA, Duke University and Howard University, among *many* others.[16]

The intellectual poison from these studies has poured into the minds of our university students for years. What is the irony of this? We're paying the Middle East professors in our universities to poison our sons and daughters with the billions of dollars America spends to fill our gas tanks. Our money is sending radical Islamic teachers to America's universities to teach our children to hate the United States of America and to hate Israel.

For the first time America is involved in a war where oil is going to determine the victim and the victor!

SECTION II
THE INTERSECTION BETWEEN BIBLE
PROPHECY AND WORLD EVENTS

Chapter 5

REBIRTH OF THE ROMAN EMPIRE: THE EUROPEAN UNION

THE REBIRTH OF THE OLD ROMAN EMPIRE IS HAPPENING before our very eyes. You see more evidence of it every day on the news, and you read it in the daily paper.

Before he died, Sir Winston Churchill said, "We must build a...United States of Europe."[1] That's becoming a reality. T. R. Reid, an American journalist and head of the London branch of the *Washington Post*, said, "At the dawn of the 21st century, a geopolitical revolution of historic dimensions is underway, the reunification of Europe."[2]

Twenty-five nations have joined together, with another dozen or so on the waiting list, to build a common economy, a government, and a culture unlike anything the world has known. Europe is more integrated today than at any other time in the Roman Empire. The world is now looking for another Caesar, another all-powerful empire that will rule humanity with a fist of iron.

That empire has been born. However, it has not come to its full brutal force, but it will. It is in its genesis element known as *the European Union*. That "Caesar" will soon come to be, and the world will call him, in due time, *the Antichrist*. His *iron-fisted control* will monitor the purchases of every person on Planet Earth for every hour of every day. No one will be able to buy a loaf of bread or a bottle of milk without it being recorded (Rev. 13:14).

A PROFILE OF DANIEL

The irony of this drama is that the prophet Daniel described it more than twenty-five hundred years ago. He told it in such detail that it is undeniable.

At the time Daniel lived, the Jewish people were nearing the end of their seventy-year captivity under the Babylonians. *Daniel* means, "God is my judge." His divine gift was the ability to understand visions and dreams and to know the unknowable. In Deuteronomy 29:29, God said He would reveal secret things to His children. He was speaking specifically to the Jewish people in this instance. God, through a divine revelation, told Daniel exactly what was going to happen, just as He told Ezekiel what would happen to Israel when it became a nation again. (See Ezekiel 38–39.)

Daniel had been captured by Nebuchadnezzar around the year 616 B.C. and was taken to Babylon, which today you will recognize to be the land of Iraq. In Babylon he was trained for palace service. Although he was brought to Babylon as a slave in chains, he rose to the rank of prime minister and lived for seventy years as an adviser to the king of Babylon. Daniel was an overcomer. He came in chains. He didn't know the language. He was a member of a hated minority. He entered Babylon with captives, but he ended up riding in chariots as a prime minister. Daniel was loved and honored by God because he maintained his integrity to the things of God.

THE KING'S MEN AND THE DREAM

In the first twelve verses of Daniel 2, we read that Nebuchadnezzar, the king of Babylon dreamed a dream—*but he forgot the dream*! The king called all his advisers, which included astrologers and sorcerers, to tell him what his dream meant. They couldn't do it. Even his magicians, who had the power to dialogue with demons by incantation, could not interpret the dream.

He asked the astrologers, who had the power to know the will of the gods and to predict the future by stars. They couldn't tell him the dream or its interpretation.

Then he asked the sorcerers, who communicate with the dead, but not even his sorcerers knew the dream or its interpretation.

It's not that these people were not motivated to give the king the information he wanted. He motivated them with these words:

> My decision is firm: if you do not make known the dream to me, and its interpretation, you shall be cut in pieces, and your houses shall be made an ash heap. However, if you tell the dream and its interpretation, you shall receive from me gifts, rewards, and great honor.
> —DANIEL 2:5–6

Now that's a motivational speech if I've ever heard one. All his men could say was, "O king, no man on earth can tell the king this answer."

In his anger, Nebuchadnezzar began to kill all the wise men. In great fear, some of them went to Daniel and said, "Help us."

So Daniel went to the king and told him that he could give him the interpretation of the dream. But he insisted that he and his companions first needed to pray. When you don't know what to do, don't call the psychic hotline—*kneel and talk to God*. He can give you the answer.

Jeremiah 33:3 says, "Call to Me, and I will answer you, and show you great and mighty things, which you do not know." The God of Abraham, Isaac, and Jacob is the God who answers prayer. Elijah prayed, and fire came from heaven. Joshua prayed, and the sun stood still. Daniel prayed, and hungry lions lay down in silent slumber.

Daniel prayed, and God gave to him the dream that another man had dreamed, and then gave to him the exact interpretation of that dream. So I'm saying to you again that prayer should not be your last chance—it should be your first choice.

NEBUCHADNEZZAR'S DREAM

Daniel's first interpretation was of the dream Nebuchadnezzar had, recorded in Daniel 2. In this dream, Nebuchadnezzar saw a great and awesome image. The head of the image was of fine gold. His breasts and arms were silver, his belly and thighs were brass, his legs were iron, and his feet were made partly of iron and partly of clay. In the dream, a stone that had never been cut by human hands smote the image on its feet and broke them in pieces. Then the stone continued by breaking into pieces and crushing the clay, the iron, the brass, the silver, and the gold. Together they became like the chaff of the summer threshing floors. The wind carried them away, and no trace could ever be found of them. Then the stone that had smote the image became a great mountain and filled the whole earth. (See Daniel 2:31–35.)

Daniel then interpreted the dream for Nebuchadnezzar.

In this dream, Daniel saw the panorama of prophecy through the end of the age. God revealed to him the nations that would enter the stage of history and the sequence in which they would appear. He also understood the personality and manner of warfare they would employ to secure their international and global dominance.

Why did God give Daniel the revelation to the dream? This is one of two times in Scripture when God gave one man the total picture of the end of the world. Daniel saw it all. If you want to know the panorama of prophecy, it's all found in Daniel chapters 2 and 7.

God gave the title deed to the land of Israel to Abraham, the father of the Jewish people, as we can read in Genesis 17:8: "I give to you and your descendants after you the land in which you are a stranger, all the land of Canaan, as an everlasting possession; and I will be their God." This covenant was with the Jewish people—with the exclusion of Ishmael, and the land of Israel was an everlasting possession.

God wanted Daniel to know that He had not broken His covenant with the Jewish people. They were going to be returned to their land. The fact is that the nations of the world are now fighting over Israel and, specifically, over the city of Jerusalem. But it is the will of God for Israel and the city of Jerusalem to be under the exclusive control of the Jewish people forever.

God does not change His mind. He says, "I am the LORD, I change not" (Mal. 3:6, KJV). God does not break covenants

(Ps. 89:34). It is the will of our sovereign God for the Jewish people to control the nation of Israel and the city of Jerusalem (Ezra 4:20; 2 Chron. 13:5).

But a tragic thing happened to the Jewish people in Daniel's day. God had promised the land of Israel to them. But for their entire adult lives, they had been in captivity. Daniel and the Jewish people were surely questioning why God had taken them out of their land. They were wondering if they would ever get back to their land, whether Israel would ever again be their possession. They wanted to know when their Messiah would come.

God gave this dream to Daniel, a Jewish prophet, so that he could tell the Jewish people and all humanity which kings and kingdoms would rule over the nation of Israel from the time of Daniel until the end of the age.

THE DREAM'S INTERPRETATION

This is the dream. Now we will tell the interpretation of it before the king. You, O king, are a king of kings. For the God of heaven has given you a kingdom, power, strength, and glory; and wherever the children of men dwell, or the beasts of the field and the birds of the heaven, He has given them into your hand, and has made you ruler over them all—you are this head of gold. But after you shall arise another kingdom inferior to yours; then another, a third kingdom of bronze, which shall rule over all the earth. And the fourth kingdom shall be as strong as iron, inasmuch as iron breaks in pieces and shatters everything; and like iron that crushes, that kingdom will break in pieces and crush all the others. Whereas you saw the feet and toes, partly of potter's clay and partly of iron, the kingdom shall be divided; yet the strength of the iron shall be in it, just as you saw the iron mixed with ceramic clay. And as the toes of the feet were partly of iron and partly of clay, so the kingdom shall be partly strong and partly fragile. As you saw iron mixed with ceramic clay, they will mingle with the seed of men; but they will not adhere to one another, just as iron does not mix with clay. And in the days of these

> kings the God of heaven will set up a kingdom which
> shall never be destroyed; and the kingdom shall not be
> left to other people; it shall break in pieces and consume
> all these kingdoms, and it shall stand forever. Inasmuch
> as you saw that the stone was cut out of the mountain
> without hands, and that it broke in pieces the iron, the
> bronze, the clay, the silver, and the gold—the great God
> has made known to the king what will come to pass after
> this. The dream is certain, and its interpretation is sure.
> —DANIEL 2:36–45

Notice that Daniel said there was a head of gold on the image in Nebuchadnezzar's dream. That head of gold was Nebuchadnezzar himself. From the head, the metals used in the image went down from silver, to brass, to iron, and finally ended with feet of clay. As they descend, they decrease in value, and they increase in strength. The symbolic lesson is that as the kingdoms walked onto the stage of world history, each would increase in military power and decrease in morality.

Each metal represents a major empire that will rule the world. The military force of each empire will be stronger than the one before it. These five kingdoms are revealed in the Bible beginning in Daniel 2:32.

1. The head of gold

The first kingdom is represented by the head of gold. Daniel 2:37–38 reveals this:

> You, O king, are a king of kings. For the God of heaven
> has given you a kingdom, power, strength, and glory;
> and wherever the children of men dwell, or the beasts
> of the field and the birds of the heaven, He has given
> them into your hand, and has made you ruler over them
> all—you are this head of gold.

The first king in the sequence of kingdoms is Nebuchadnezzar. His kingdom was the first empire to rule over the Jewish people. Nebuchadnezzar conquered Jerusalem in 616 B.C.

2. The chest and arms of silver

The second kingdom was represented by a chest and arms of silver. This is the Medeo-Persian Empire. The two arms symbolize two nations: the Medes and the Babylonians. They united with the Persians to form the second great world empire.

3. The belly and thighs of bronze

The third empire represented in the image was brass. This is Alexander the Great, whose empire began in 334 B.C. Two hundred seventy years after Daniel wrote his vision of the future, Alexander the Great and his army marched to Jerusalem. As he neared the city, the high priest of Israel went out to meet Alexander and read to him and his army the writings of Daniel, which described the military techniques of Alexander the Great.

Alexander was so impressed that he said, "I'm not going to destroy Jerusalem." Instead, he went into the temple to worship. Alexander the Great, 270 years after the fact, recognized the accuracy of the Jewish prophet Daniel. Alexander the Great died at the age of thirty-three. He divided his kingdom into four parts, each with one of his commanding generals.

While he ruled, Alexander made Greek the world language. Greek is the most exact language on the earth. Greek was the language used to write the New Testament, which avoided any misunderstandings of its meaning.

I believe that God allowed Alexander the Great to conquer the world so that the New Testament could be written in Greek. In that way it became the most exact writing on the face of the earth. If you read the original text as it was given, you will comprehend its meaning.

4. The feet of iron and clay

The fourth kingdom that comes into power is the Roman Empire. Rome ruled the world with an iron fist. Rome crushed all previous empires, but it collapsed from within because of moral decay. If you follow the rise and fall of Rome, you will see a picture of how America has risen and how we are now falling.

The feet of Nebuchadnezzar's image were made of iron and clay. Iron and clay are substances that will not mix. I believe the iron is interpreted to be *democracy*, and the clay is interpreted to be *radical Islam*—two substances that will not blend. In describing the feet to Nebuchadnezzar, Daniel was saying that the last world government would be represented by a *theocratic dictatorship* and *democracies*.

Daniel described the ten toes in the feet of the image, also made of iron and clay. Those ten toes represent ten governments. The last world government before the second coming of Christ will consist of ten governments. For the first three and a half years of the tribulation period, these ten governments will rule. Then the Antichrist will arise and conquer three of those ten governments and rule the world with an iron fist.

In the Book of Revelation, we read of a beast with seven heads and ten crowns. (See Revelation 13:1.) Seven heads are mentioned because the Antichrist had conquered three nations and now ruled seven.

5. The stone in Nebuchadnezzar's dream

In Daniel 2:45, the stone becomes a great mountain and smites the image. The stone hit the image with such force that it was pulverized. Daniel said that the image became like the wheat of the summer on the threshing floor. It was literally atomized.

The stone cut without hands is Jesus Christ. Jesus Christ is the cornerstone in Zion. That's why the Bible says, "On this rock I will build My church, and the gates of Hades shall not prevail against it" (Matt. 16:18).

In Daniel's interpretation of the king's dream, he said that in the days of the kingdoms represented by the toes, the God of heaven will set up a kingdom that will never be destroyed. It will break all the other kingdoms into pieces and will consume them. His kingdom will stand forever.

When we pray the Lord's Prayer, we pray: "For thine is the kingdom, the power and the glory forever." The Bible says of Christ: "Of the increase of His government and peace there will be no end" (Isa. 9:7). When Jesus Christ, the stone cut without hands, comes back to Earth, He's going to annihilate the governments of the world, and He Himself will set up

His kingdom. It will become an eternal kingdom and will never end.

WHAT THIS MEANS IN TODAY'S WORLD

Even an uninformed person can see that the globe on which we live is racing toward a final conflict. All of humanity—every world government included—is looking for ways to destroy anyone who disagrees with the specific governing mandates in which they believe. There is a clash of civilizations just over the horizon.

What is going to happen? What's going to be the end of all this? God has always given man free will. It's not God's will—it is man's sinful, uncontrollable, demonically driven will that makes this nightmare become a reality.

But in the final analysis, God is going to say, "I'm letting you have your opportunity. You've rejected My message. You've rejected My Son, so I'm going to let you have your messiah, your Caesar, the Antichrist. And he's going to set up a kingdom.

"But when he sets up that kingdom, I'm going to annihilate it. When it's done, I'm going to set up a kingdom that will never end!"

And of His kingdom there will be no end.
—Luke 1:33

Chapter 6

BEGINNING THE ROAD
TO ARMAGEDDON

THE NATION OF ISRAEL SITS IN THE CENTER OF WORLD conflict today, as it has from the time when God gave the land of Israel to Abraham, Isaac, and Jacob through an *eternal* covenant. God Almighty created Israel by a sovereign act. Israel stands forever. The covenant between God and the Jewish people will never be broken.

> For the LORD your God will bless you just as He promised you; you shall lend to many nations, but you shall not borrow; you shall reign over many nations, but they shall not reign over you.
>
> —DEUTERONOMY 15:6

> Then I will establish the throne of your kingdom, as I covenanted with David your father, saying, "You shall not fail to have a man as ruler in Israel."
>
> —2 CHRONICLES 7:18

> Should you not know that the LORD God of Israel gave the dominion over Israel to David forever, to him and his sons, by a covenant of salt?
>
> —2 CHRONICLES 13:5

> I will make the lame a remnant,
> And the outcast a strong nation;
> So the LORD will reign over them in Mount Zion
> From now on, even forever.
>
> —MICAH 4:7

Iran believes that the property of Israel belongs to the Arab nations. It is determined to destroy Israel. They are sponsoring two armies on the borders of Israel—Hamas and Hezbollah— that are slowly but surely attacking Israel with Iranian-sponsored weapons. Why? Because radical Islam believes they have a mandate from Allah to kill Christians and Jews, and to take dominion over Israel, especially Jerusalem.

You may have observed this conflict in the Middle East and wondered, "Why should I be so concerned about Israel?" As a Christian, you should be concerned because Israel is the gateway of blessings for you, for your children, for your ministry, for your business, and for the United States of America.

GOD'S PROMISE TO BLESS THOSE WHO BLESS ISRAEL

Consider the blessings of God in the Old Testament to those who blessed Israel and the Jewish people. Consider the two pharaohs in the life of Joseph. The pharaoh who blessed Joseph was blessed of God and became the most prosperous leader in all of the world in his generation. The pharaoh who "knew not Joseph" and tormented the Jewish people came into judgment. (See Exodus 1.) He was drowned in the Red Sea and turned to fish food, because those who bless Israel are blessed, and those who curse Israel are cursed.

> Now the LORD had said to Abram:
>
> "Get out of your country,
> From your family
> And from your father's house,
> To a land that I will show you.
>
> I will make you a great nation;
> I will bless you
> And make your name great;
> And you shall be a blessing.
>
> I will bless those who bless you,
> And I will curse him who curses you;
> And in you all the families of the earth shall be blessed."
> —GENESIS 12:1–3

Those verses contain God's promise for all time.

Consider the story of Jacob and Laban. Jacob, a Jewish man, was working for a Gentile by the name of Laban, who was his father-in-law. When Jacob told Laban that he wanted to take his family and return to his own country, Laban begged him to stay: "Please stay . . . for I have learned by experience that the LORD has blessed me for your sake" (Gen. 30:27). God blessed the Gentile Laban because of the life of Jacob.

Consider the blessings in the New Testament. When Jesus of Nazareth began His public ministry, His healing ministry spread far and wide. In Luke 7, a Roman centurion who had a sick servant wanted to find out how to get Jesus to come to his house so his servant could be healed.

If you read the story, you will find that the Jewish elders came to Jesus to tell Him of the kindness of this centurion. They said that the centurion "loves our nation, and has built us a synagogue" (Luke 7:5). Upon hearing of the Gentile's kindness, Jesus went with him and healed his servant. Because the Gentile centurion did something practical to bless the Jewish people and the nation of Israel, Jesus was willing to pray for his servant.

Consider the outpouring of the Holy Spirit in the tenth chapter of Acts on the house of Cornelius. Why was the house of Cornelius the very first house chosen to receive the gospel message and to be filled with the Holy Spirit? You find the answer in Acts 10:22: "And they said, 'Cornelius the centurion, a just man, one who fears God and has a good reputation among all the nation of the Jews, was divinely instructed by a holy angel to summon you to his house, and to hear words from you.'" Cornelius was of good report among the Jewish people.

Are you? Listen to Jesus's request in Matthew:

> When the Son of Man comes in His glory, and all the holy angels with Him, then He will sit on the throne of His glory. . . . Then the King will say to those on His right hand, "Come, you blessed of My Father, inherit the kingdom prepared for you from the foundation of the world: for I was hungry and you gave Me food; I was thirsty and you gave Me drink; I was a stranger and you took Me in; I was

naked and you clothed Me; I was sick and you visited Me; I was in prison and you came to Me."

Then the righteous will answer Him, saying, "Lord, when did we see You hungry and feed You, or thirsty and give You drink? When did we see You a stranger and take You in, or naked and clothe You? Or when did we see You sick, or in prison, and come to You?" And the King will answer and say to them, "Assuredly, I say to you, inasmuch as you did it to one of the least of these My brethren, you did it to Me."

—MATTHEW 25:31–40

I have often heard Christians say, "I would do anything for Jesus." Would you do what He asked? Jesus asked you to bless the Jewish people and the state of Israel. Jesus said, "You are My friends if you do whatever I command you" (John 15:14). In another place, He said, "Why do you call Me 'Lord, Lord,' and not do the things which I say?" (Luke 6:46). The question is: Do you want the favor of God enough to do what Jesus Christ asks you to do?

God has asked us to bless the nation of Israel and the Jewish people. When you do something personal to bless the state of Israel or the Jewish people, you are honoring the life of Christ.

Do you want to receive financial blessings that you cannot contain? When you are facing the pain at the pump, you need the blessing of God. Bless the nation of Israel and the Jewish people.

Do you want a supernatural breakthrough like the Roman centurion wanted for his sick servant? Then bless the nation of Israel and the Jewish people.

THE VALLEY OF DRY BONES

As Ezekiel 37 opens, Israel has been in captivity for hundreds of years. God took Ezekiel (in a vision) to a great valley full of dry bones (Ezek. 37:2). These bones had been dead for a very long time.

As we look at this passage's meaning today, we can recognize that God was talking about the nation of Israel. In Ezekiel

37:11–12, we read: "Son of man, these bones are the whole house of Israel. They indeed say, 'Our bones are dry, our hope is lost, and we ourselves are cut off!' Therefore prophesy and say to them, 'Thus says the Lord GOD: "Behold, O My people, I will open your graves and cause you to come up from your graves, and bring you into the land of Israel."'" It was hard for Ezekiel to believe that the dry bones could live again, but God promised to open their Gentile graves and bring them out of captivity into the land of Israel.

On May 15, 1948, the miracle promise of God became a reality. The mighty right hand of God gathered the Jewish people from sixty-six Gentile nations, and the state of Israel was reborn, just as Bible prophecy said it would happen.

Every Jewish person who returns to live in Israel makes Israel a greater and stronger nation and fulfills the prophecies of the Old Testament prophets. The partners of John Hagee Ministries have helped bring thousands of Jews home to Israel, and I thank them for their sacrificial obedience to God's Word.

All Bible directions are given as they relate to Israel. In the mind of God, Israel is the center of the universe. Jerusalem is the city of God. God sent the prophet Ezekiel to the Jewish people in captivity to remind them that God would restore Israel.

To understand how Bible prophecy relates to our world today, it is very important to grasp the fact that God promised to deliver the Jewish people out of captivity. They had been in captivity for hundreds of years when He made that promise. It seemed absolutely preposterous to think that there would be a moment of deliverance. Yet He promised to regather His chosen people from the nations of the world and bring them back to Israel.

> For I will take you from among the nations, gather you out of all countries, and bring you into your own land. Then I will sprinkle clean water on you, and you shall be clean; I will cleanse you from all your filthiness and from all your idols. I will give you a new heart and put a new spirit within you; I will take the heart of stone out of your flesh and give you a heart of flesh.
> —EZEKIEL 36:24–26

BEGINNING THE ROAD TO ARMAGEDDON

The current generation is witnessing global warfare—and the weapon of war is *oil*. Israel has been reestablished as a nation. Russia has recently invaded Georgia and is defying America and the West. The International Atomic Energy Agency (IAEA) now believes that Syria is operating a secret nuclear program. In a report posted on CBC.com on June 22, 2008, Gregory L. Schulte, chief U.S. delegate to the IAEA, told the Associated Press:

> Syria was caught withholding information from the IAEA. Now Syria must disclose the truth about Al Kibar and allow IAEA's inspectors to verify that there are no other undisclosed activities.[1]

As I stated earlier, Iran is racing toward nuclear weapons and promises to wipe Israel off the map. President Ahmadinejad has made it clear he also intends to attack America.

The road map to Armageddon begins in Ezekiel 38. In Ezekiel 38 we begin to hear about the war of Gog and Magog:

> And the word of the LORD came unto me, saying, Son of man, set thy face against Gog, the land of Magog, the chief prince of Meshech and Tubal, and prophesy against him.
>
> —EZEKIEL 38:1–2, KJV

Who is Gog? Gog is a dictator of a nation to the far north of Israel. In *Jerusalem Countdown* I explained how we can identify this land to be the nation of Russia. Ezekiel 38:1–2 tells us that Gog was "chief prince" of the land of Magog. *Chief*, which means "head," is the Hebrew word *Rosh*. In his ancient Hebrew lexicon, the great Hebrew scholar Gesenius (1786–1842) identified *Rosh* as an ancient name for Russia. To further support that this is Russia, in his book *The Destiny of Nations*, Dr. John Cumming said: "The King of the North I conceive to be the autocrat of Russia…that Russia occupies a place and a very momentous place, and the prophetic word has been admitted by almost all expositors."[2]

Ezekiel 38:4 says, "I will turn you around, put hooks into your jaws [keep that phrase in your mind], and lead you out, with all your army." God is saying to the king of the north, "I'm going to put a hook in your jaw and drag you to the hills of Israel." As I stated earlier, I believe that the hook in the jaw is oil. Without oil, no military superpower can fight. Their planes can't fly. Their tanks can't move. And without those two implements, their machinery of war stops.

The hook is something that forces a fish to go in a certain direction toward the fisherman. The fish has no choice. The hook overpowers the fish and compels him to obey the fisherman. The fisherman here is God Himself. And that hook is oil!

Verse 5 goes on to identify the armies that will come with Russia. It clearly speaks of "Persia," modern-day Iran. That has never changed. It also identifies the nation of "Ethiopia," which today represents the African Islamic nations, and speaks of "Libya."

Verse 6 names "Gomer," which is Germany. In today's unstable global climate, anti-Semitic feelings against the Jewish people are exploding in Germany. Verse 6 also mentions "Togarmah," which is Turkey, also a hotbed of terrorism.

These nations together with Russia come against Israel in the Gog-Magog war at some time in the future. And that future is very near. Never in the history of the world have all of the players been on the stage at the same time. When my father was teaching this in the middle 1940s, there was no state of Israel, and Russia was starving to death. The Arab nations were living in deep poverty, but oil has brought them immense wealth. With that immense wealth, there has been an explosion of radical Islam. Russia now has a partner in war—radical Islam, and is ready and willing to help Islam with its design to control the world.

We are now facing a war between Israel and Iran. The four nations described by Ezekiel are Russia, Libya, Germany, and Turkey. All will be crushed by the hand of God when they attack Israel. (See Ezekiel 38.)

BIBLE PROPHECY INTERSECTING WITH HISTORY

Think about this: thousands of years ago, a Jewish prophet under the anointing of the Holy Spirit wrote exactly what was going to be happening in the twenty-first century so accurately and in such detail that it is more accurate than what you read in today's newspapers.

Russia, which presently has four states greatly influenced by Muslims, will lead an Islamic army against Israel. When are they going to do that? Ezekiel 38:8 says, "In the latter years." I believe that means after Israel was reborn, referring to 1948. Ezekiel 38:9 says, "You will ascend, coming like a storm, covering the land like a cloud, you and all your troops and many peoples with you."

In other words, there will be such a vast Islamic army led by the former Soviet Union, or Russia, that it will look absolutely hopeless for Israel. Consider the power of Islam around the world. Today, 60 of the world's 184 countries are considered part of the house of Islam. Islam dominates the Middle East.[3]

The Islamic faith is growing in Africa, Asia, Europe, and in the United States. One report states:

> A manifestation of the demographic Islamisation of the Western world, there are now over a thousand mosques and Islamic centres in the United States alone. And the country has professional associations for Muslim engineers, Muslim social scientists and Muslim educators. There are some six million American Muslims, and the number is rising impressively. It can no longer be seen as Islam versus the West. It is Islam and the West or Islam in the West, as some observers have noted.[4]

How did this happen? Muslims living in countries around the globe are funded by the vast resources of Arab oil money. Muslims are building mosques at such a rate that many Muslims claim England will soon be the first Muslim European country.

As we have stated already, President Ahmadinejad of Iran has promised to wipe Israel off the map if he can get his hands on nuclear weapons. But I have to say this: Even if he gets them, he has a much greater enemy than the United States of America and Israel. God Almighty is watching from heaven, and His integrity is based on defending Israel and the Jewish people.

> "And it will come to pass at the same time, when Gog comes against the land of Israel," says the Lord GOD,

"that My fury will show in My face. For in My jealousy
and in the fire of My wrath I have spoken: 'Surely in
that day there shall be a great earthquake in the land of
Israel, so that the fish of the sea, the birds of the heavens,
the beasts of the field, all creeping things that creep on
the earth, and all men who are on the face of the earth
shall shake at My presence.'"

—EZEKIEL 38:18–20

God Almighty is saying, "I'm going to go to war against the
enemies of Israel. It's enough! I'm furious with the terrorists. I'm
furious with the human bombers who have murdered innocent
women and children in synagogues. I'm furious with the abuse
Israel has had to endure from the nations of the world. My wrath
is going to be poured out on the enemies of Israel."

In Ezekiel 39:2–7 we read the result of God's wrath:

"I will turn you around and lead you on, bringing
you up from the far north, and bring you against the
mountains of Israel. Then I will knock the bow out of
your left hand, and cause the arrows to fall out of your
right hand. You shall fall upon the mountains of Israel,
you and all your troops and the peoples who are with
you; I will give you to birds of prey of every sort and to
the beasts of the field to be devoured. You shall fall on
the open field; for I have spoken," says the Lord GOD.
"And I will send fire on Magog and on those who live
in security in the coastlands. Then they shall know that
I am the LORD. So I will make My holy name known
in the midst of My people Israel, and I will not let them
profane My holy name anymore. Then the nations shall
know that I am the LORD, the Holy One in Israel."

In the King James Version, verse 2 reads: "And I will turn thee
back, and leave but the sixth part of thee…" God will destroy
85 percent of this mighty army as a testimonial that He is the
almighty God of Abraham, Isaac, and Jacob who defends Israel.
The sixth that remain will know who the great I AM truly is.

The results will be so devastating that it will take Israel seven
months to bury the dead and seven years to burn the weapons
of war. God's whole purpose for bringing this judgment to pass

is: "Then shall they know that I am the LORD their God" (v. 28, KJV).

Today, for the first time in human history, all the players are on the stage. Russia, Iran, all of the Islamic nations are there. Look at what is happening in the world; this battle could take place any day.

THE JUDGMENT OF THE NATIONS

When Jesus returns to Earth, the first thing that will happen is the judgment of the nations. The basis for the judgment of each nation will be made by determining how that Gentile nation treated the Jewish people.

> I will also gather all nations,
> And bring them down to the Valley of Jehoshaphat;
> And I will enter into judgment with them there
> On account of My people, My heritage Israel,
> Whom they have scattered among the nations;
> They have also divided up My land.
> —JOEL 3:2

When you read what God is going to do in the judgment, you understand that every anti-Semite who tormented Israel and the Jewish people is going to pay with his eternal soul. Obadiah 15–16 (NLT) says:

> The day is near when I, the LORD,
>   will judge all godless nations!
> As you have done to Israel,
>   so it will be done to you.
> All your evil deeds
>   will fall back on your own heads.
> Just as you swallowed up my people
>   on my holy mountain,
> so you and the surrounding nations
>   will swallow the punishment I pour out on you.
> Yes, all you nations will drink and stagger
>   and disappear from history.

Where will America stand in that judgment?

A MESSAGE FOR OUR JEWISH FRIENDS

This message is important to our Jewish friends because the God of Abraham, Isaac, and Jacob has sworn to defend Israel. When you see this battle approaching, do not fear. The Holy One of Israel is with you. You are still the apple of His eye. You are the chosen people. God delivered you from Pharaoh. He delivered you from Haman's plot. Hitler could not blot you out, and Ahmadinejad will not "wipe you off the map." Your greatest victory, O house of Israel, is right before you. The God of Abraham, Isaac, and Jacob is with you. God Himself will annihilate your enemies.

> "Neither will I hide my face any more from them: for I have poured out my spirit upon the house of Israel," saith the Lord GOD.
>
> —EZEKIEL 39:29, KJV

Chapter 7

HAS WORLD WAR III BEGUN?

In Matthew 24:3, Jesus's disciples asked Him, "Now as He sat on the Mount of Olives, the disciples came to Him privately, saying, 'Tell us, when will these things be? And what will be the sign of Your coming, and of the end of the age?'"

Technically speaking, there is not going to be an end to the world. But there will be an end to the world *as we know it*. The world has changed since 9/11. The world that existed in America before is gone forever. But I assure you, when nuclear weapons start falling, it will be the end of the world as we know it for everyone.

In the Book of Revelation, the Bible is very clear in its teachings that God is going to re-create the world to make it like the Garden of Eden. Man will have so polluted the earth with nuclear proliferation that it will have to be re-created for man to reinhabit. Man is doing his absolute best to destroy the beautiful world that God made, but God will re-create it.

IMPORTANT QUESTIONS TO ASK

This chapter answers the following:

1. What is the definition of *world war*?
2. Has World War III begun?
3. Why does radical Islam hate us?
4. What's going to happen next?

What is the definition of *world war*?

World war is defined as the combined fight involving the major nations of the world against a specific cause or common enemy. In World War I (1914–1918), the United Kingdom, France, Belgium, Serbia, Montenegro, the Russian Empire, and the United States, along with twenty-one other nations, allied against the central powers of the empires of Germany, Austria-Hungary, the Ottoman Empire, Bulgaria, and three other countries.

In World War II (1939–1945), America, the United Kingdom, Poland, France, Canada, and the Soviet Union were allies in a fight against Nazi Germany, Fascist Italy, and Japan. The world was at war.

Has World War III begun?

The battle for the survival of Western civilization is now engaged. The Islamic Republic News Agency recently reported Iran's President Ahmadinejad stating that Israel "was on the verge of disappearing."[1] In today's world, a nation can disappear only through a nuclear holocaust. You can be sure that as soon as Iran has nuclear weapons, they will be used against Israel and then the United States of America.

Recently, a British master spy, Eliza Manningham-Buller, shocked the world by saying, "British spies are watching 1,600 people in 200 cells believed to be plotting terrorist acts in Britain or overseas."[2] Get those numbers in your mind. In *Jerusalem Countdown*, I tell you of an FBI report that identifies eight U.S. cities that radical Islam has targeted to be blown up simultaneously.[3] The purpose for these potential threats is Islam's desire to crush the will of the American people for resisting the rule of radical Islam.

In June 2008, Ahmadinejad said this: "Today, the time for the fall of the satanic power of the United States has come and the countdown to the annihilation of the emperor of power and wealth has started!"[4]

These simple facts, coupled with the phenomenal growth of radical terrorist acts around the world, lead to no other conclusion than that World War III has begun. This war is between the democracies of the free world and radical Islamics. President Bush said, "This nation is at war with radical Islamic fascists."[5]

Iran is swimming in oil money. It has the ability to buy nuclear power from North Korea any day of the week. Islamic terrorists were arrested in Canada with three times the explosives used in the Murray building in Oklahoma City. Their objective was to capture Canada's prime minister and cut his head off.[6] That was an act of war.

Spain is at war with radical Islam. On March 11, 2004, bombs exploded on three commuter trains in Madrid, killing more than two hundred people and injuring fourteen hundred.[7] Islamic leaders told Spain to take their troops out of Iraq. Spain bowed to the demands of radical Islam immediately.

On October 18, 2008, China agreed to sell two new nuclear reactors to Pakistan, a country that traded its nuclear know-how and technology with Iran, Libya, and North Korea.[8]

Throw in the radical Islamic attacks in Afghanistan, Yemen, Kuwait, the Philippines, Egypt, Turkey, Bangladesh, and Thailand, and it is easy to determine that, indeed, the world is at war. These nations are at war against a common enemy. It is the clash of kingdoms. It is a clash that will not stop until one enemy defeats the other.

Why does radical Islam hate us?

Why was America attacked on 9/11? Why does radical Islam hate us? It's not only because of our support of Israel. Radical Islam hates us because it is their religious duty to hate us. Remember, I said, "Radical Islam."

Radical Islam is a doctrine of death. Judeo-Christianity is a doctrine of life. For radical Islamist fascists, it is their desire, their hope, their ambition, and their highest honor to die for Allah.

For radical Islamists, an *infidel* is a Christian or a Jew, or anyone who does not believe in Islam. Radical Islam teaches their children from birth to love death, just as we love life. Knowing these facts means you can begin to understand something about the mind-set of radical Islam.

Sheikh Mohammed Yazbek stated after the bombing of

the U.S. Marine's battalion headquarters in Lebanon: "Let America, Israel, and the world know that we have a lust for martyrdom and our motto is being translated into reality."[9]

They hate us because we are free. Radical Islam hates freedom. They want to turn the clock back to the dark ages of the seventh century.

Islam calls Jewish people *apes* and *pigs*. They call Christians *those who incur Allah's wrath*. Anyone who is not a follower of Islam must either convert or be killed. Radical Islam cannot survive in an atmosphere of freedom.

The women of radical Islam have no freedom. They cannot go to school, drive a car, or have an opportunity to work in a public job. The man has the right to punish his wife, literally whip her, if he wishes. He may divorce her for any reason and may put her out of his home, penniless.

On Fox News recently there have been some reports about the concept of *honor killings* among Muslims.[10] Honor killings are happening in America, but they have been happening in the radical Islamic faith for centuries.

In July of 1977, an Englishman with a miniature camera was able to take a photograph that shocked the world. It was the public execution in Jeddah of Princess Misha'al Mohammed and her boyfriend.[11] She was shot six times in the head, and he was beheaded. Western governments hurried to suppress the showing of the film.

Dave Hunt, one of the great prophecy writers in America, wrote these words:

> When Muhammad died in A.D. 632, much of Arabia, having been forced to embrace this new faith by the sword, tried to defect thinking that they had the right to quit Islam when they wanted to. They had forgotten the words of Muhammad passed on from Allah, "Whoever relinquishes his faith, kill him."[12]

In other words, whoever tries to quit the church, kill him. During the years of A.D. 630 to A.D. 632, in obedience to Allah's command to behead apostates, Muhammad's successor and father-in-law, with what he called *holy Muslim warriors*, killed seventy thousand former Muslims. When you kill seventy thousand people because they try to quit your church, that's not peaceful.

Abu Bakr went forth with his troops and said, "Command them, those who try to quit Islam, to reembrace Islam. But if they refuse, do not spare any of them. Burn them with fire and kill them with force and take the women as prisoners."[13]

That's not peaceful, but it is a fact of history. Radical Islam is not peaceful. I want to make this very clear. There are Islamic people who want peace, but I'm talking about a radical Islam that is determined to see Western civilization destroyed.

In Saudi Arabia, the practice of any religion other than Islam is strictly prohibited, just as it was in the lifetime of Muhammad. Yet Saudi Arabia is building mosques in America from coast to coast with the billions of dollars that Americans are sending them through our gas tanks. Saudi Arabia has what Hitler was trying to produce—a nation where Jewish people cannot even enter because they are considered to defile the soil when they touch it with their feet. This is radical hatred.

As I've already stated, Saudi Arabia has accomplished what Hitler dreamed of—a Jew-free society. Saudi Arabian officials have promised that they will continue to support Palestinian terrorism against Israel and America. In April of 2002, from a government mosque, a sheikh of the Saudi Arabian government said this: "I am against America until this life ends.... She is the root of all evil and wickedness on the earth."[14]

He continued with these words: "Muslim brothers in Palestine, do not have any mercy, neither compassion on the Jews.... Their women are yours to take.... God made them yours.... Why don't you wage jihad? Why don't you pillage them?"[15] My friend, that is not peaceful.

We, the people of the United States, must recognize this: There is a war being waged by a very determined enemy—radical Islam—to destroy us and to take our country down. We, the people, must stand boldly and persistently until freedom is defended in our generation.

What's going to happen next?

Many people are asking, "What is going to happen next in the Middle East?" Russia has just invaded Georgia. Russia is going to continue to behave in a very aggressive and hostile manner toward NATO and every NATO nation. They will be increasingly hostile to the United States of America, because we are the superpower that Russia hates most.

Russia is trying to control the world's oil. That's why they're in Georgia. They want to control the oil pipeline, and they want to have a seaport with direct access to Russia. Russia will continue to ingratiate itself to Iran and to other radical Islamic nations. Why? Because Russia wants the oil to become a superpower.

Radical Islam wants the military prowess and guidance from Russia to enable it to conquer Israel and Jerusalem. Those two powerful forces are merging for the purpose of destroying the nation of Israel. Russia will lead a huge Islamic army against Israel. But God is going to crush that army. It will be such a devastating defeat for Russia and the Islamic nations that their military power will be destroyed forever.

We have the opportunity to watch these events unfold in world news, but it was revealed to us by Daniel and Ezekiel twenty-five hundred years ago. What you can read for yourself in Bible prophecy is more accurate than what you will see on the evening news telecasts.

The war for America's survival has begun. Few in America are willing to admit it. Few are willing to address it. But radical Islam is prepared for this battle to last as many as fifty or a hundred years. Americans want a war to be over in six weeks or six months. There is great division in the country now because the war in Iraq has lasted more than four years. This is a new day with a different enemy and a different warfare.

We must understand that the price of freedom demands a relentless determination to defend freedom. Let America heed the words of Winston Churchill, who, in the dark days of World War II, said this: "You ask, what is our aim? I can answer in one word: It is victory, victory at all costs, victory in spite of all terror, victory, however long and hard the road may be; for without victory, there is no survival."[16]

For those of us in America, victory has to be our theme. Victory in spite of the terror. Victory in spite of how long and how hard the road may be in this battle against global terrorism. Without victory, there is no survival of this nation for you, for your children, or for your children's children.

May God preserve the freedom of the United States of America, where we enjoy life, liberty, and the pursuit of happiness every day.

SECTION III
GOD'S SECRETS FOR
AVOIDING YOUR PERSONAL
ECONOMIC CRASH

Chapter 8

WHAT DO I DO NOW?

I UNDERSTAND THAT AT TIMES THE THUNDER OF OUR fears keeps us from being able to hear the still, small voice of God. So before we go any further, let's address some of the critical concerns I know every American has about his or her financial security in today's economic crisis.

I want you to know how these world events are going to affect your personal finances. The Bible outlines God's economic system and helps us to see what God has to say about what's happening *right now in our world*. His advice will help you to avoid the devastation of personal financial collapse

The Bible supports the concept of doing one thing well:

> Brethren, I do not count myself to have apprehended; but one thing *I do*, forgetting those things which are behind and reaching forward to those things which are ahead, I press toward the goal for the prize of the upward call of God in Christ Jesus.
> —PHILIPPIANS 3:13–14

If you are focused on that "one thing" God has called you to reach, God will direct you to opportunities that will meet your every need in any crisis. God told Elijah to go to the house of the widow woman and, "I will feed you *there*." The place of God's purpose is the place of God's power. Find God's purpose for your life, and discover God's power and abundance received in your life.

1. What is the first thing I should do?

The most important thing you can do to be prepared for financial freedom today and for the future is *reduce debt*. This is the first thing I did—personally and in my church. In chapter 9, I will discuss the danger of debt and help you to understand the importance of doing everything you can to rid yourself of personal debt. One of the ways you can do this is to find opportunities to create additional income.

I recently observed this principle in action through the example of a man whom we hired to utilize his farm equipment to bale hay on our ranch. My son, Matthew, also observed this man working to put a roof on someone's home. He asked, "What are you doing roofing? I thought you were a rancher."

The response was one that every one of us should take to heart. He replied, "I'm doing whatever I need to do, wherever and whenever I can, to earn a little extra money." Take that advice to heart. Don't sit on your blessed assurance; create additional income opportunities for yourself for the purpose of reducing debt. Start with your smallest debt; pay it off, and keep on going until you are debt free. You didn't get in debt overnight, and you won't get out overnight, but *today* is the day to get started.

2. What should the small-business owner be doing to protect his business from financial disaster?

There are four important steps that you should be taking to protect your business. First, do everything you can to *reduce your overhead*. Tighten up the ship…put stopgap measures in place to spend less and conserve more. Second, you should be *strengthening your relationships with staff, clients, vendors, business associates, and financial institutions*. This is the time to pull together—build relationships that create an environment of support and initiative for you and from you to others. Third, now is the time for you to *distinguish and differentiate your product*. Now is *not* the time for you to be just like dozens of other small companies who are producing exactly what you are producing. What makes you different? Why should people be coming to you for your product instead of to someone down the street? Use this opportunity to distinguish who you are and what you contribute with your product that no one else can. Finally, now is the time for you to *diversify*. Do this with your services, with your product, and with your strategies. Follow the rancher's advice: do whatever you need to do, wherever and whenever you can, to create new opportunities for your business. Use this time to improve your business.

3. What action should the person take who is close to retirement and worried that his or her retirement savings will be jeopardized by plummeting Wall Street investments held through a 401(k)?

First of all, this person—and every Christian in America—should be putting their faith and trust in God's economic system revealed through His Word. "Faith without works is dead" (James 2:20). Point: You work your way out of debt. Nothing will work in your life until you do. I also think it is prudent to weather the storm. Stay put—the market will correct itself. Most pension funds do not respond well to early liquidation. It is more important for you to listen to what God is telling you to do than to follow the advice of people. You already have "inside information" from God about how to stay financially free of debt and financial collapse; review His principles, and stand firm in your faith in His provision.

4. What creative measures can churches or organizations take to help out members or employees who have lost homes, possessions, or jobs in this crisis?

There are practical measures churches and organizations can take to provide support for those who need it most. Cornerstone is providing its staff with an opportunity to eat lunch on campus for only three dollars. Not only is this saving lunch money, but it's also saving gas money for our staff. But we are expanding this opportunity in other ways as well. We offer a three-dollar dinner (with kids under twelve eating free) before our weeknight prayer service. In this way, we are reaching families who would not have been able to come to this event without this help, thereby increasing attendance. We are doing whatever we can at the most practical level during this crisis.

At the same time, we are teaching our congregation that *godly* benevolence begins with the individual—not with the church or government. Paul teaches:

> Honour widows that are widows indeed. But if any widow have children or nephews, let them learn first to shew piety at home, and to requite their parents: for that is good and acceptable before God.... But if any provide not for his own, and specially for those of his own house, he hath denied the faith, and is worse than an infidel.... If any man or woman that believeth have widows, let them relieve them, and let not the church be charged; that it may relieve them that are widows indeed.
> —1 TIMOTHY 5:3–4, 8, 16, KJV

Paul says that a family member who does not provide for his own is "worse than an infidel." At Cornerstone, we teach the "bottom-up" principle of benevolence. It begins with the individual. In the kingdom of God, God looks at the individual as the highest form of governance. If an individual cannot supply his or her own needs, the next step is that the individual receive support from his or her family. If there is no opportunity for a family member to help with the need of the individual, and/or the family is overwhelmed, should that person receive help from the church? In God's economic system, it is the civil government's responsibility to *protect* individuals—not to *support* them.

Cornerstone provides financial seminars and financial counseling, and finds them to be very successful. The seminars afford preventive measures against reckless spending, while the counseling provides accountability through teaching and discipleship.

As we are reinforcing God's principles for benevolences, we are also teaching God's principles of tithing. In Malachi 3:10, God says: "'Bring the whole tithe into the storehouse, that there may be food in my house. Test me in this,' says the LORD Almighty, 'and see if I will not throw open the floodgates of heaven and pour out so much blessing that you will not have room enough for it.'" We will discuss this more in chapter 11, but what if God threw open "the floodgates of heaven" and poured out His blessing upon a church in direct proportion to the number of people in that church who tithed? We believe in the importance of training people to obey God's principle of tithing. It is those tithes that will enable a church to do the work of the Lord—including the ministry of benevolence.

GOD'S ECONOMY SYSTEM

God has given us an investment manual to use to find the answers to our questions about what is going on in our world. He understands our panic that our own personal finances will collapse and thrust us into an economic nightmare. God's Investment Manual—*the Word of God*—is the finest investment manual on earth. I want to introduce you to the finest investment counselor who ever walked the face of the earth—Jesus of Nazareth.

He gave thirty-eight parables that are included in the Word of God. Sixteen of the thirty-eight teach us how to manage our possessions. In the New Testament, there are five hundred verses on prayer and five hundred verses on faith. But there are more than two thousand verses on how to achieve financial freedom.

Read with me one of the biblical principles for your financial freedom:

> Give, and it will be given to you: good measure, pressed down, shaken together, and running over will be put into your bosom. For with the same measure that you use, it will be measured back to you.
> —LUKE 6:38

God's Investment Manual is filled with principles for handling finances. As we dig into God's Word, we find that there are basic rules by which we make our economic decisions.

Albert Mohler, president of the Southern Baptist Theological Seminary, has made some wise observations about our Christian view of this economic crisis:

> Christians should think seriously about this economic crisis and ponder what it would mean to come to a Christian understanding of what it means to be participants in this economy....Christians should look at the

economy as a test of our values. The Bible values honest labor and dedicated workers, and so should we. The Bible warns against dishonest business practices, and we must be watchful. False valuations are, in effect, lies. Dishonest accounting practices are just sophisticated forms of lying. Insider information is a form of theft. The Bible honors investment and thrift, and Christians must be wary of the impulse for short-term gains and pressure for instant profit.[1]

We will consider some of these issues in this section of this book. What can you and I do to protect ourselves from the looming financial and economic crash? God's Word gives counsel that will lead you to financial freedom and supernatural abundance. It reveals God's economic system for financial freedom.

As you read, remember that God has promised to bless His people. Rest assured that God is in control. You can have peace—and financial security—even when the economy collapses around you. Rather than hit the panic button, concentrate on finding ways to glorify God in the way you live and address your economic concerns. Trust our Master Investment Counselor—He will never let you down.

Chapter 9

PROSPERITY IS A CHOICE

T HERE ARE SECRETS IN THE WORD OF GOD THAT WILL lead you to financial freedom and supernatural abundance. These principles will cause your business to succeed. They will take your personal prosperity to levels that will stagger your mind!

Would you like to have total financial freedom? In today's climate of economic disaster, and a looming crisis over oil that threatens to lead us to the prophetic fulfillment of Bible prophecy for the end of the world, many Christians are confused about how to obtain financial freedom. What are the factors that produce financial freedom?

It's difficult to tell! Each week when you stop in at your local gas station to buy gas, the price per gallon seems to be rising through the roof. Then suddenly prices fall again, bringing with it a false sense of security, only to skyrocket once more. When you stop in the local convenience store to pick up some bread, you get stuck in a long line of people waiting to buy lotto tickets. Is luck the way to financial freedom? I think not!

For years you have probably been told that the safest place for your money is in your local bank. Yet today financial institutions across America—large and small—are crumbling and threatening Americans with a financial crash greater than our grandparents experienced during the Great Depression.

This is not the way to financial freedom.

The stress over money—and the lack of it—is the number one reason many marriages crumble.

Remember this: failure cannot happen in your life without your permission. Success is a choice based on the wisdom of God's Word. You make the decision to live in poverty or prosperity every day of your life!

SEVEN CHOICES THAT WILL GUARANTEE YOUR POVERTY

There are seven choices you can make that God's Word says will guarantee your poverty.

1. You vote for poverty when you buy anything on a credit card that you cannot pay off before the end of the month.

   The rich rules over the poor,
   And the borrower is servant to the lender.
   —PROVERBS 22:7

2. You vote for poverty when you go to the bank and agree to be the personal guarantee for someone else for any reason.

   A man devoid of understanding shakes hands in a pledge,
   And becomes surety for his friend.
   —PROVERBS 17:18

3. You vote for poverty when you steal *God's tithe*. Your business and your resources will be under a curse, and your income will never be enough.

   You are cursed with a curse,
   For you have robbed Me,
   Even this whole nation.
   —MALACHI 3:9

4. You vote for poverty when you steal either time or resources from your employer or from your neighbor. Theft brings poverty, and God cuts you off! Your choices demand God's judgment!

Then he said to me, This is the curse that goes out over the face of the whole land; for everyone who steals shall be cut off…

—Zechariah 5:3, amp

5. You vote for poverty when you can work, but won't work. The average workweek in the Bible was sixty hours; if you are working forty hours, you're working part-time.

The soul of a lazy man desires, and has nothing;
But the soul of the diligent shall be made rich.

—Proverbs 13:4

6. You vote for poverty when you throw away something of value. Do you waste things?

And the younger of them said to his father, "Father, give me the portion of goods that falls to me…the younger son…wasted his possessions with prodigal living.

—Luke 15:12–13

7. You vote for poverty if you are anti-Semitic. Every anti-Semitic act is a decision for poverty, and every act of blessing and kindness toward the Jewish people is a choice for prosperity.

I will bless those who bless you,
And I will curse him who curses you;
And in you all the families of the earth shall be blessed.

—Genesis 12:3

Many Christians get very pious when money is mentioned. If you're too pious to talk about money, you're so heavenly minded you are no earthly good. Are you living in lack? Look at your choices. You are casting a vote for poverty or prosperity by your actions, every day of your life. Choices have consequences.

I call heaven and earth as witnesses today against you, that I have set before you life and death, blessing and cursing; therefore choose life, that both you and your descendants may live.

—Deuteronomy 30:19

If it were wrong for you to enjoy material blessing, then why did God give them to David or Solomon or to His Son, Jesus Christ?

God said to David, "I took you from the sheepfold, from following the sheep, to be ruler over My people, over Israel" (2 Sam. 7:8).

God prospered Solomon:

> The weight of gold that came to Solomon yearly was six hundred and sixty-six talents of gold, besides that from the traveling merchants, from the income of traders, from all the kings of Arabia, and from the governors of the country.
>
> —1 Kings 10:14–15

At today's value of gold, Solomon's income well exceeded $65 million per year. I would certainly call him a wealthy man!

If wealth and abundance are not good, why would God give them to His Son?

> Worthy is the Lamb who was slain
> To receive power and riches and wisdom,
> And strength and honor and glory and blessing!
>
> —Revelation 5:12

GREAT WISDOM PRODUCES GREAT WEALTH

I started working when I was eight years old. My mother hated laziness like the devil himself, and she found a job for me picking cotton for one dollar per hundred pounds of cotton picked. Some of my friends didn't think that the way to financial freedom was picking cotton, but I had no choice.

At the age of eight, I wasn't a rocket scientist, but I was bright enough to know that a gallon of water weighed about eight pounds. The second day as a cotton-picker, I went into the fields with a sixteen-foot cotton sack—and the biggest jug of water I could carry. You guessed it! I poured the water on the cotton...this is not wisdom—it is a commonsense way of leveraging your assets.

But listen to Solomon, the wisest man in history and one of the wealthiest, tell you the value of wisdom:

> Happy is the man who finds wisdom,
> And the man who gains understanding;
> For her proceeds are better than the profits of silver,
> And her gain than fine gold.
> She is more precious than rubies,
> And all the things you may desire cannot compare with her.
> Length of days is in her right hand,
> In her left hand riches and honor.
> Her ways are ways of pleasantness,
> And all her paths are peace.
> She is a tree of life to those who take hold of her,
> And happy are all who retain her.
> —PROVERBS 3:13–18

Do you get the message? Great wisdom produces great wealth! Wisdom is better than silver or gold. It is better than rubies. It brings long life, riches, and honor. It brings peace and happiness to all. It is better than any other thing you could desire.

What is wisdom? Webster defines *wisdom* as: "evidence of possession of inside information that produces good judgment."

Let's look into the pages of world history and learn from men who transformed facts (knowledge) into a fortune!

Mayer Amschel Rothschild

Mayer Rothschild (1743–1812) was born in Frankfurt, Germany. He was a rabbinical student who discovered that his brilliance in the area of finance was world-class.

He began buying and selling rare coins. In 1769 he became the financial agent for Prince William IX, grandson of George II of England. Soon Rothschild was the deal maker between the major banks of Europe.

Mayer Rothschild's fortune was made in just a few days because of secret knowledge he obtained. His great opportunity came during the Battle of Waterloo between Napoleon and Wellington of England. It was a battle to see who would rule Europe.

Early in the battle, Napoleon and France appeared to be winning. However, Wellington, with help from the Prussians, turned the tide of battle in favor of England. On June 18, 1815, Rothschild, who had his agent at the battlefront, received the news by carrier pigeon that England had won.

However, the London Stock Market—the Wall Street of Europe—believed England had lost. Their information was coming by courier on horseback—far slower than carrier pigeon. The London stock market crashed!

Within a few hours, with his special knowledge that England had actually won, Rothschild bought the wealth of Europe for pennies on the dollar. He had complete control of the British economy and forced England to set up a new bank of England—which his son Nathan Rothschild controlled.

From there, Rothschild set up five banks in Europe, putting his five sons in charge. The Rothschild family controlled the wealth of Europe for two hundred years.

How did that happen? A man with inside information had the courage to take bold action based on his sound judgment of the situation.[1]

Failure can only happen with your permission. Success and prosperity do not just happen; success is organized, thought out, and executed. Success demands discipline and persistence. Start today!

Noah

Noah is another example of a man who had inside information and whose sound judgment saved his family and the world. Noah knew the future—God told him what it was. God had become so angered by the wickedness of man on the earth that He told Noah, "The end of all flesh has come before Me, for the earth is filled with violence through them; and behold, I will destroy them with the earth" (Gen. 6:13).

But Noah "found grace in the eyes of the LORD" (v. 8), and God had a plan of protection for Noah. "I will establish My covenant with you; and you shall go into the ark—you, your sons, your wife, and your sons' wives with you" (v. 18).

With the inside information Noah received from God, in faith he took bold action: he built an ark. That action based on his knowledge saved his family, while the rest of the world was destroyed.

Great wisdom creates great wealth!

Joseph

Consider Joseph; he knew the future because of the dreams God gave him. He knew there would be seven years of abundance followed by seven years of famine. He took bold action and built grain storage facilities. Because of his wise response to the inside information he received from God, and God's supernatural supervision, Joseph saved his family (the Jewish nation) and all of Egypt, and he made Egypt the richest nation on earth.

GOD'S INSIDE WISDOM FOR YOUR FINANCIAL SECURITY

What inside information do you have about the future that can benefit your family in a time of worldwide economic crisis? By looking in God's Word, we can look into the future today.

An important verse of Scripture for you to remember is this:

> The secret things belong to the LORD our God, but those things which are revealed belong to us and to our children forever, that we may do all the words of this law.
> —DEUTERONOMY 29:29

The Bible clearly states that the greatest worldwide economic crash in history is coming.

The Book of James describes this economic crash that will happen "in the last days."

> Come now, you rich, weep and howl for your miseries that are coming upon you! Your riches are corrupted, and your garments are moth-eaten. Your gold and silver are corroded, and their corrosion will be a witness against you and will eat your flesh like fire. You have heaped up treasure in the last days. Indeed the wages of the laborers who mowed your fields, which you kept back by fraud, cry out; and the cries of the reapers have reached the ears of the Lord of Sabaoth. You have lived

on the earth in pleasure and luxury; you have fattened
your hearts as in a day of slaughter.

—JAMES 5:1–5

The worldwide news that has been blaring from our televi-
sions and radios and written in our newspapers during the past
few months and weeks have shown us evidence of this *insider
knowledge* revealed in the Book of James.

Economists the world over are scrambling to try to understand what is happening, and the media are attempting to
explain to the average Americans who are fearing the worst. On
September 25, 2008, ABC journalist Betsy Stark said this:

> Even if ordinary Americans are still not able to connect
> the dots of how the malfunctioning of markets they
> can't see or understand has morphed into a crisis of epic
> proportions, they are getting the message about where
> this all could lead if Congress doesn't cut a deal: Stocks
> will tank, nest eggs will crumble, retirement dreams will
> disappear, lending will halt, people will not be able to
> buy houses, home prices will fall some more, foreclo-
> sures will rise some more, consumers will hunker down,
> corporate profits will sink, jobs will be lost…and those
> are consequences everyone can understand.[2]

Read the following headline news breaking recently:

On September 30, *USA Today*'s headline read: "Dow
PLUNGES 778: Parties Point Fingers as Rescue Fails." The
article continued: "The failure of the $700 billion bailout
Monday send S&P 500 to its worst percentage loss since
October 1987 and cost investors 1.2 trillion."

The *Wall Street Journal*'s headline on October 10, 2008,
read: "Market's 7-Day Rout Leaves U.S. Reeling"…and
continued by saying, "Stocks in a slow-motion crash as Dow
drops another 679 points. After year of declines, investors lose
$8.4 trillion of wealth."[3]

New York Times writer Vikas Bajaj states on October 15, 2008:
"Bail Out of Banks Becomes Buy-In—White House Confirms
Government Will Invest $250 Million." His article continued:

- What's Going On: In a reversal of its stance, the Treasury Department will purchase shares in Banks.

- What It Does: Temporarily guarantees more than $1.5 trillion debt and insures $500 billion in business deposits.

- The Cost: $250 billion injection into banks total bill will be $2.85 trillion, more than three times the original $700 billion bailout package

On October 15, 2008, the *Wall Street Journal*'s headline read: "While The World Is Listening, Brown Touts Global Oversight." The article states: "As the British bank-bailout plan becomes a model for Europe and the U.S., U.K. Prime Minister Gordon Brown is using his new platform as financial statesman to push what he sees as the next step: a global system of financial supervision."[4]

These headlines are troubling to the secular world, yet for the wise Christian who is carefully studying God's Investment Manual, the Bible, we knew this economic crash was coming and had the opportunity to follow our Master Investor's instructions for choosing the blessing of God over the poverty of man.

Today's decisions are tomorrow's destiny.

CAN THIS WORLDWIDE ECONOMIC CRASH HAPPEN NOW?

Every person should realize that the present economic meltdown on Wall Street created by the collapse of Lehman Brothers, bank mergers, the crash of Freddie Mac and Fannie Mae via the greed manifested in the subprime lending scam, the desire of Russia to control Europe's oil supply, the power of China to control the U.S. economy, and the refusal of the U.S. Congress to control spending will eventually crush the economic engines of our nation and the world.

The billions of American tax dollars that our government has just thrown into an economic inferno has only postponed the verdict of a massive global economic crash and probably made it more severe and far reaching.

If you believe that the next Congress will stop earmarks, wasteful spending, greed, and corruption in legions of projects loaded with cost overruns that our children and grandchildren will be taxed to their eyebrows to pay for...then you see a world I don't see.

Let's connect the dots and have the courage to recognize reality.

1. Our government is on an unstable fiscal path with a national debt that is approaching ten trillion dollars. It will soon require a majority of the taxes the IRS collects to pay the interest on the national debt.

2. As America's baby boomers retire and health costs continue to rapidly rise along with the cost of Social Security, Medicare and medical programs will cost billions of dollars the American economy simply does not have.

3. The projected cost of all federal programs will exceed available financial resources. If Congress does not bring program costs in line with available taxes, budget deficits will become so large that the U.S. government will not be able to borrow enough to fund the cost of government.

   Translation? The government will be broke, and there will be no source of money to fix the problem in any series of proposed emergency meetings by G-7 or anyone else.

   How long do we have to get our house in order? Some experts predict from eight to ten years if Congress gets aggressive and nothing else happens on America's horizon to plunge us deeper into debt.

4. The prophet Haggai describes a future economic crash with runaway inflation. Haggai writes: "You have sown much, but you have reaped little; you eat, but you do not have enough; you drink, but you do not have your fill; you clothe yourselves, but no one is warm; and he who earns wages has earned them to put them in a bag with holes in it" (Hag. 1:6, AMP).

Note the pictorial description of a man putting his money "in a bag with holes in it." It makes no difference how much money you make, the money will run through the holes in the bag faster than you can make it. That's the perfect description of runaway inflation. It's coming!

5. James describes an economic crash that will happen in the last days in James 5:1–5. "Come now, you rich, weep and howl for your miseries that are coming upon you" (v. 1)! I challenge you to read this section of Scripture and know that this is something in the future. It's coming!

6. The prophet Daniel in chapter 8 describes the characteristics of the coming Antichrist. None of the descriptions is more relevant than Daniel 8:26, which states, "Through his policy also he shall cause craft to prosper in his hand."

Why would this charismatic world dictator need to make craft or industry to prosper on a worldwide scale if there was not a global economic problem? This is something that is clearly coming in the future, which means that the global economic problems are not over by any means. You have insider information. Get ready!

THE DANGER OF DEBT

One man said, "I'm going to live within my means, even if I have to borrow to do it." This man clearly did not understand the danger of debt. We can understand the danger by reading God's Word.

> The rich rules over the poor,
> And the borrower is servant to the lender.
> —PROVERBS 22:7

A borrower is anyone living on bank loans and credit cards. If this describes you, then you have become the servant of anyone who has lent you money. Romans 13:8 advises, "Owe no one anything." If it is necessary for you to borrow anything, when it is due—*pay it and pay it on time*!

Psalm 37:21 gives a caution that we should all observe: "The wicked borrows and does not repay." This means two things:

1. It refers to a borrower who never pays.
2. If you don't pay on time, God numbers you with the *wicked*.

Why does God identify a borrower who never pays or pays late with *wickedness*? It is because you have lied to your creditor. When you agreed to the credit terms, you in essence said, "I'll pay you on the date the bill is due." In addition, because you have not paid according to the credit terms, *you are stealing the creditor's produce*—using it for your benefit at his expense. Pay on time!

Debt will keep you from providing for your family. It can lead to intense arguments and will put stress on your marriage. Debt in marriage has led to spousal and child abuse.

Debt is not sin—but it is very dangerous!

In Bible times, your creditor could claim your children or send you to "debtor's prison." Fact: This still happens. Debt brings stress, anger, depression, fear, and regret over the bills you cannot pay. It puts you in an emotional prison.

CREATING YOUR PERSONAL PHILOSOPHY TOWARD DEBT

There are five kinds of debt that we should be aware of:

1. Credit card debt, whose interest is called "usury" in the Bible (Prov. 28:8)

2. Consumer debt
3. Mortgage debt
4. Investment debt
5. Business debt

Before going into debt of any kind, ask yourself these five questions:

1. "Do I need this?"

Always carefully consider the *need* before you go into debt. Are you really responding to a critical need, or are you responding to your own carnal *greed*? God will help you meet your *needs*!

There are many things that you can do to help meet the need. For example, have you ever had a garage sale? How can you recycle some of the things you no longer use to meet your need? How many times have you asked yourself, "What in heaven's name did I buy that for?"

You will be surprised at how successfully you can reduce your *greed* so that you can clearly respond only to your *need*.

2. "Does my spouse *agree* with me about taking on this debt?"

The Bible states, "Can two walk together, unless they are agreed?" (Amos 3:3). If you and your spouse do not have unity in the way you spend your money—or incur your debts—when the *bill comes due,* there is going to be a fight.

Make certain that you and your spouse agree about money matters.

3. "Do I have peace about this new debt?"

Unless you have peace about a purchase you are about to make, don't make it. Ask yourself: "What positive contribution will this purchase make to my life? Will it make me happier? Will it make my life more stressful, or will it give me peace?"

In this current climate of great economic unrest, every American is thinking about his own financial future. The Bible has promised us that God is with us. The Bible has given us principles that ensure God's blessing on every part of our lives—including our financial security.

We can have peace in the midst of an economic storm. Let peace reign in your life by keeping your eyes focused on God, our Master Investor. He promises:

> You will keep him in perfect peace,
> Whose mind is stayed on You,
> Because he trusts in You.
>
> —ISAIAH 26:3

4. "How am I going to pay this back?"

You should no more step blindly into a major financial purchase without knowing how you are going to pay back the debt than you would step blindfolded off a cliff.

Think and plan carefully and realistically for how you are going to pay back the debts you incur. Don't be thinking foolishly: "If I give up foolish things like food…clothes…car …then I can afford this!" Instead, ask: "What am I and/or my family going to do without if I make this purchase?"

5. "What goals am I meeting with this debt that could be met in *no other way*?"

Get creative with your needs! There are many ways that you may be able to meet a need that you or a family member has without going into debt.

THE SPIRITUAL DANGER OF DEBT

Be aware that there is a great spiritual danger to debt! I've seen people forsake their relationship with God because of their debt. They buy a house that costs more than they can pay for, they buy a car that is above their means, they buy clothes, jewelry, and luxuries they don't need with money they don't have (on credit). They sink themselves into debt and end up losing their jobs. Then they get bitter at God because their car gets repossessed or they lose their homes. When the bills arrive, they take their debt to God and plead or demand that their debt be paid. When He doesn't respond as they deem fit, they turn their back on God and reject Him for His failure to meet their need. When you go into long-term debt, be sure you are not being presumptuous with God. The Bible warns, "Do not boast about tomorrow, for you do not know what a day may bring forth" (Prov. 27:1).

This very point is one of the looming threats in our current economic crisis. Thousands of Americans have had homes they shouldn't have purchased foreclosed on because they assumed, "My next twenty-five years will be better," "I'll have a great job in a couple of years," or "My health is great, and there won't be any problems I can't handle so that I'll be able to pay for all of this."

During the *boom* years recently in the housing business, many buyers went into high debt and took on shaky mortgages to buy a home.

> Homeownership has increased by 5 percent during the last 5 boom years and is now at a record high of 70 percent. Lenders made it almost impossible for a potential homebuyer to get turned down for a mortgage. Suddenly, borrowers with questionable credit, who would have never been able to get a loan ten years ago, were getting mortgages without breaking a sweat.[5]

Currently, as of June 2008, we have more than 1.75 million homes in foreclosure. The whole of 2007 had 1.5 million homes in foreclosure—up 53 percent from 2006.

Be careful about the purchases you make. Don't lose your relationship with God as a result of looming debt.

America is in deep financial trouble because of debt. Our national debt as of October 15, 2008, at 09:25:05 PM GMT is $10,297,691,671,523.66 and climbing.[6] For the first time in our history, the International Monetary Fund has sent a letter to the U.S. government stating that America's debt could destabilize the world economy.[7] Even the New York City Debt Clock has run out of digits![8]

There is a great imbalance of world trade imports and exports. America now owes other nations more than they think we can pay back. As a result, foreign markets are pulling their money out of Wall Street and putting it in European markets.

The best way to avoid personal debt that leads to spiritual consequences is to remember this: Beware the danger of debt! Borrow to buy only what you're willing to lose.

Chapter 10

GIVERS GAIN

A YOUNG LAD OF SIXTEEN YEARS, NAMED WILLIAM, LEFT home to seek his fortune, with all his possessions tied in a bundle carried in his hand. While in New York, he met an old canal-boat captain. William told the captain that his father was too poor to keep him, and the only trade he knew was soap and candle making.

The old man then knelt and prayed earnestly for the boy and advised: "Someone will soon be the leading soap maker in New York. It can be you as well as someone else. Be a good man, give your heart to Christ, and pay the Lord all that belongs to him."

William took the old man at his word, and as soon as he earned his first dollar, he gave one-tenth of it to God. From that moment on, he considered that ten cents of every dollar were sacred to the Lord. He continued to have regular employment, and soon he became a partner in his employer's business. Later he became the sole owner.

He gave the Lord one-tenth of all his income. The business grew, so he began giving two-tenths, then three-tenths, four-tenths, five-tenths, and finally he gave all his income.

This young man's name was William Colgate, who has given millions to the Lord's cause.[1]

William Colgate chose to give his money to the work of the Lord rather than hoarding it for his personal use. That's a lesson we all need to learn if we want to avoid a personal economic crash. God honors those who give.

GOD IS A GIVER

God gave His most precious gift—Jesus Christ. "For God so loved the world that He gave His only begotten Son, that whoever believes in Him should not perish but have everlasting life" (John 3:16). Because He gave, salvation is free to you and me, but it almost bankrupted heaven.

Jesus Christ, God's Son, gave His life for you. As the words of a well-known song say so powerfully:

> He paid a debt He did not owe.
> I owed a debt I could not pay.[2]

God has given His best to you and me. He has given everlasting life. He daily gives to each one of us the breath that we breathe (Job 33:4). He gives us strength to get out of bed and go to work (Ps. 27:1). He gives us health and healing: "By His stripes we are healed" (Isa. 53:5). He has given to us the keys the kingdom (Matt. 16:14). He has given us power over sin and Satan (Rom. 8:2) and has blessed us with the gift of His precious Holy Spirit (Acts 2:38).

When you get to heaven, He will give you a golden crown, a dazzling white robe of righteousness, and a mansion built by the Architect of the ages. He will give you a new name by which you will be called in your new home in the New Jerusalem (Rev. 3:12).

God gave His Son, and the Son gave every drop of blood in His veins—*what are you giving*? Giving is the only proof you have that the cancer of greed has not consumed your soul.

The Bible promises a four-way gain to those who give:

> Give, and it will be given to you: good measure, pressed down, shaken together, and running over will be put into your bosom. For with the same measure that you use, it will be measured back to you.
>
> —LUKE 6:38

When you give to God, He gives you back a gain that is:

- Given in good measure
- Pressed down

- Shaken together
- Running over

And that, my friend, is a good financial return.

GIVING IS LEARNED

We are not born with the natural instinct and desire to give; giving is a learned behavior. Giving doesn't come naturally.

A mother wanted to teach her daughter a moral lesson. She gave the little girl a quarter and a dollar for church. "Put whichever one you want in the collection plate, and keep the other for yourself," she told the girl. When they were coming out of church, the mother asked her daughter which amount she had given. "Well," said the little girl, "I was going to give the dollar, but just before the collection the man in the pulpit said that we should all be cheerful givers. I knew I'd be a lot more cheerful if I gave the quarter, so I did." Experts say you must do at least something twenty-one times before it becomes a habit. Begin to give; try God, and He will be true to His Word (Mal. 3:10–12).

The Bible says, "God loves a cheerful giver" (2 Cor. 9:7). As you are learning to give, learn to give with a cheerful heart.

GOD'S GIVING BELONGS ONLY TO HIS CHILDREN

An important principle about God's giving is found in the New Testament. God's giving is reserved for His children.

> Therefore let no one boast in men. For all things are yours....And you are Christ's, and Christ is God's.
> —1 Corinthians 3:21, 23

> ...and if children, then heirs—heirs of God and joint heirs with Christ.
> —Romans 8:17

We are not *equal* heirs with Christ, which would mean we share equally. Half would be His, and the other half ours. The verse says that we are *joint heirs*. All He has is mine, and all I have is His! What a deal!

God delights in the prosperity of His children. He clearly

states, "Beloved, I pray that you may prosper in all things and be in health, just as your soul prospers" (3 John 2). Notice that there is a connection between your *soul* and your *prosperity*.

Our prosperity is assured if we will follow the principles of God's Investment Manual—the Bible. Joshua 1:8 says, "This Book of the Law shall not depart from your mouth, but you shall meditate in it day and night, that you may observe to do according to all that is written in it. For then you will make your way prosperous, and then you will have good success."

PRINCIPLES FOR GIVING FROM GOD'S INVESTMENT MANUAL

God's Investment Manual is filled with principles about your prosperity. Take the time to reflect here on just a few.

> Blessed is the man
> Who walks not in the counsel of the ungodly,
> Nor stands in the path of sinners,
> Nor sits in the seat of the scornful;
> But his delight is in the law of the LORD,
> And in His law he meditates day and night.
> He shall be like a tree
> Planted by the rivers of water,
> That brings forth its fruit in its season,
> Whose leaf also shall not wither;
> And whatever he does shall prosper.
>
> —PSALM 1:1–3

> And you shall remember the LORD your God, for it is He who gives you power to get wealth.
>
> —DEUTERONOMY 8:18

> The wealth of the sinner is stored up for the righteous.
>
> —PROVERBS 13:22

> Let them shout for joy and be glad,
> Who favor my righteous cause;
> And let them say continually,
> "Let the LORD be magnified,
> Who has pleasure in the prosperity of His servant."
>
> —PSALM 35:27

The blessing of the LORD makes one rich,
And He adds no sorrow with it.

—PROVERBS 10:22

Evil pursues sinners,
But to the righteous, good shall be repaid.

—PROVERBS 13:21

Honor the LORD with your possessions,
And with the firstfruits of all your increase;
So your barns will be filled with plenty,
And your vats will overflow with new wine.

—PROVERBS 3:9–10

Are you a child of King Jesus? If you are, then act like it...think like it...live like it...*and give like it*! God rewards the giver with prosperity.

GIVERS CONTROL THEIR FINANCIAL FUTURE

The story is told in 1 Kings 17 about the widow who fed Elijah during a famine in the land.

> Then the word of the LORD came to him, saying, "Arise, go to Zarephath, which belongs to Sidon, and dwell there. See, I have commanded a widow there to provide for you." So he arose and went to Zarephath. And when he came to the gate of the city, indeed a widow was there gathering sticks. And he called to her and said, "Please bring me a little water in a cup, that I may drink." And as she was going to get it, he called to her and said, "Please bring me a morsel of bread in your hand." So she said, "As the LORD your God lives, I do not have bread, only a handful of flour in a bin, and a little oil in a jar; and see, I am gathering a couple of sticks that I may go in and prepare it for myself and my son, that we may eat it, and die." And Elijah said to her, "Do not fear; go and do as you have said, but make me a small cake from it first, and bring it to me; and afterward make some for yourself and your son. For thus says the LORD God of Israel: 'The bin of flour shall not be used up, nor shall the jar of oil run dry, until the day the LORD sends rain on the earth.'" So she went away and did according to the word of Elijah; and she and

he and her household ate for many days. The bin of flour
was not used up, nor did the jar of oil run dry, according
to the word of the LORD which He spoke by Elijah.
—1 KINGS 17:8–16

Think about this story. The people were starving to death.
This widow woman and her only son had just enough for a
small cake to eat, and then, "We will die!" Elijah showed up at
her house and said, "Give me the bread."

I wonder how you and I would respond in such a circum-
stance. This woman immediately gave what she had to the
prophet—and as a result her flour bin and jar of oil were
supernaturally filled to the brim. They had enough to eat—and
more—for as long as they needed it.

She gave what she possessed to receive what she did not
possess. What do you need? What you give to God will determine *when* His blessing arrives and *how much* arrives. Your
sacrificial giving will secure your financial future.

It is a fact that when you open your hand toward God, God
opens His hand toward you. Your seed may leave your hand—
but it will never leave your life! It goes into your future, where
God multiplies it thirty...sixty...and one hundredfold.

Your seed is the *only* influence you have over your financial
future. Remember God's promise to open His hand to you
when the offering is taken in your church.

Today's decisions are tomorrow's *realities*. Give God what is
right—not what is left!

GIVE WHAT IS IN YOUR HAND

The widow woman gave what was in her hand! What do you
have in your hand? Whatever you have in your hand to give is
what God will use to *create* your future!

Our Investment Manual gives us an example of a man who
was willing to use what was in his hand, and as a result he
led an entire nation—God's chosen people—to personal and
financial prosperity and to freedom. In the Book of Exodus, we
have the story of Moses—whom God called to be the liberator
of Israel. Who was Moses? Moses was:

- The man to face down Pharaoh (Exod. 8:9)
- A man who would talk to God (Exod. 4:1)
- The man to receive the Ten Commandments (Exod. 34:28)
- A man to change the course of history (Acts 3:22)

What did God ask Moses to do that determined his future? The story begins with this interchange between God and Moses:

> So the LORD said to him, "What is that in your hand?" And he said, "A rod." And He said, "Cast it on the ground."
>
> —EXODUS 4:2–3

Moses had a worthless shepherd's stick in his calloused hand, but he gave it to God, and God used it to *create* a new and glorious future for Moses. That rod turned into a serpent in Pharaoh's court that attacked and killed the serpents of Pharaoh's sorcerers, Jannes and Jambres. (See Exodus 7:8–12.) In doing so, God, through Moses, crushed the occult power of Egypt with a shepherd's stick.

That same rod was placed into the Nile River, and as a result, the waters of the Nile turned to blood, flowing from Pharaoh's palace to the sea. Every river…every stream…every bathtub in Egypt was caked with blood.

That rod was dipped into the Red Sea and the waters parted. As a result, the children of Israel escaped from Pharaoh's bondage. When Pharaoh's army set out in pursuit of the Israelites, every soldier in Pharaoh's army—along with horses, chariots, and weapons—was covered over by the raging waters of the Red Sea. Every horse and rider drowned. (See Exodus 14.) Moses gave his simple shepherd's staff to God, and God used it to supernaturally set free an entire nation.

In the hand of Moses, that rod struck a dry rock, and millions of gallons of water gushed out in the desert to refresh the Hebrews and water their cattle.

Moses obeyed God and gave Him what he had in his hand. God anointed the rod and crushed the occult powers of an entire nation, overcame Pharaoh and his military powers, liberated Israel, and brought living water to a thirsty nation.

What do you have in your hand? Choose today to release it to God, *and watch what He is able to do with what you have in your hand.* Give it to God. He can use it to set the captive free, to refresh the nations, and to create your future. Give it to God, and watch the parade of miracles. Give it to God, and financial freedom is yours!

Remember this: when your seed leaves your hand (even if it's a simple stick), your harvest leaves the warehouse of heaven and heads toward you.

GOD WANTS YOU TO INVEST IN YOURSELF

Some of the best investment advice that God, our Master Investor, gives to His children is this:

> Do not lay up for yourselves treasures on earth, where moth and rust destroy and where thieves break in and steal; but lay up for yourselves treasures in heaven, where neither moth nor rust destroys and where thieves do not break in and steal. For where your treasure is, there your heart will be also.
> —MATTHEW 6:19–21

The day is going to come when all you will have is what you have given to God!

Christians often confuse the meanings of two words:

1. Self-interest
2. Selfishness

It is a good thing to have *self-interest*. For example, it is in my self-interest to accept Jesus Christ as my personal Savior. It assures me of eternity with Him in heaven. The only options we have for eternity are *heaven* or *hell*. You don't have to be a rocket scientist to know that heaven is the right choice.

It is in my self-interest to be happy. The Bible gives me principles that will help me to make the choice to choose happiness.

> A merry heart does good, like medicine.
> —PROVERBS 17:22

> The joy of the LORD is your strength.
> —NEHEMIAH 8:10

Rejoice in the Lord always. Again I will say, rejoice!
—Philippians 4:4

INVEST IN THINGS THAT ARE PERMANENT

Jesus taught us to invest wisely! Invest in things that are permanent! Dewdrops are as pretty as diamonds until the sun comes out, and they disappear. Jesus taught us that it's not in our self-interest to invest in something that moths can eat or that rust can decay or that thieves can carry off.

The Bible teaches us that, "Heaven and earth will pass away, but My words will by no means pass away" (Matt. 24:35). Earth and the things of Earth *are not permanent*. If I told you that your house was going to burn down in two hours, would you get all your valuables and put them in the house? No! That would be insane! You would immediately get all your valuables out of the house.

The Bible guarantees that the earth will burn with fire. In 2 Peter 3:10, we read:

> But the day of the Lord will come as a thief in the night,
> in which the heavens will pass away with a great noise,
> and the elements will melt with fervent heat; both the
> earth and the works that are in it will be burned up.

Invest your time and money wisely in things that are permanent. Invest in the kingdom of God. Lay up treasures for yourself that are eternal!

Why is it critical to understand the importance of giving? It is because God has created a universe where it is impossible to *receive* or *prosper* without giving! If something within you resents giving, that something is not of God.

> You have sown much, and bring in little;
> You eat, but do not have enough;
> You drink, but you are not filled with drink;
> You clothe yourselves, but no one is warm;
> And he who earns wages,
> Earns wages to put into a bag with holes.
> —Haggai 1:6

Givers gain! You do not qualify to receive from God—or from Neiman Marcus—until you give. If you walk into Neiman Marcus and see a T-shirt you like, until you give the man the money for the shirt, you do not receive the shirt. If you take the shirt without first giving... you are shoplifting!

When you go to the store and select fifty dollars worth of groceries, you give the man fifty dollars and walk out with a sack of groceries so small you can throw it in the glove compartment of your Toyota.

The Bible commands, "Give, and it will be given to you" (Luke 6:38). Until you give, you don't qualify to receive.

Learn this Bible investment principle: God Almighty controls the economy—and your income. Our source is not the government. It's not a rich aunt or a trust fund. God is our source. "And you shall remember the LORD your God, for it is He who gives you power to get wealth" (Deut. 8:18). God controls your income; there is no such thing as "fixed income." In the kingdom of God, your income is controlled by your giving.

REASON GIVERS AND REVELATION GIVERS

There are two kinds of givers: *reason* givers and *revelation* givers. A reason giver is controlled logically by his mind. He does not ask God how much he should give. He asks his CPA, and the CPA consults the IRS code and says, "You've given too much already. Buy another certificate of deposit."

A revelation giver is controlled by the Holy Spirit. He sees God as his source. He does not give according to what he has but according to what God can supply. He understands that the earth is going to pass away. And he knows the value of his soul—which is the length of eternity. He knows the day is coming when all he will have is what he has given to God. A revelation giver knows the divine principle of Luke 6:38.

If your harvest is not big enough, it's because you are planting a small handful of seed and expecting a barn full of wheat. This is not possible! Attack your lack!

To givers, God gives a lasting memorial. In Matthew 26:13 we read, "Assuredly, I say to you, wherever this gospel is preached in the whole world, what this woman has done will also be told as a memorial to her."

This verse is telling the story of the woman who broke open the alabaster box of costly perfume and poured it over the head, beard, tunic, and robe of Jesus. That costly perfume represented an entire year's wages, yet she freely gave it to Jesus. Its powerful aroma filled the house.

It was a massive sacrifice for her, and it brought to her the criticism of those watching what she was doing. Judas, the disciple who would betray Jesus, complained about it to Jesus, saying, "She should have used the money to give to the poor."

It's a fact that anytime you do something special for God, there will be a Judas who will criticize you.

But she gave a gift that kept on giving. When Jesus wept in the Garden of Gethsemane, the aroma of that perfume was still there, saying, "Someone loved You enough to give their very best."

When Judas kissed Him in betrayal, Jesus felt the pain of betrayal—but that aroma was still saying, "Someone loved You enough to give their very best." When He was tied to Pilate's whipping post and His flesh torn off His body by the blows of the nail-studded cords of the whip the soldiers used to beat Him, that aroma was saying, "You are not forgotten; someone loved You enough to do their very best."

And as He was nailed to the cross, that aroma was there. When Roman soldiers gambled for His robe, they smelled that aroma, which was crying out, "Someone loved this man...loved Him totally...loved Him enough to give their very best!"

Do you love Jesus enough to give Him your very best? If you do, and you want God's financial blessing, make a pledge to Him today to release what is in your hand, allowing God to use it to shape your future.

Remember this: what you give to God determines what God will give to you.

Chapter 11

HOW TO QUALIFY FOR FINANCIAL FREEDOM

W HEN YOU WALK INTO A BANK AND ASK FOR A MORTGAGE loan to buy a new home, you have to qualify for the loan first. You can't buy a ten-million-dollar mansion if you are only making ten dollars an hour!

When you apply for the university, you must first qualify for acceptance. You can't go to MIT with a string of Fs on your report card.

A student told his English teacher, "I don't think I deserve that F."

"I don't think you deserve the F either," the teacher responded. "However, that's the lowest grade we give around here."

How do you qualify with God for financial freedom? You qualify by giving God your tithes.

> "Will a man rob God?
> Yet you have robbed Me!
> But you say,
> 'In what way have we robbed You?'
> In tithes and offerings.
> You are cursed with a curse,
> For you have robbed Me,
> Even this whole nation.
> Bring all the tithes into the storehouse,
> That there may be food in My house,
> And try Me now in this,"

Says the Lord of hosts,
"If I will not open for you the windows of heaven
And pour out for you such blessing
That there will not be room enough to receive it.
And I will rebuke the devourer for your sakes,
So that he will not destroy the fruit of your ground,
Nor shall the vine fail to bear fruit for you in the field,"
Says the Lord of hosts;
"And all nations will call you blessed,
For you will be a delightful land,"
Says the Lord of hosts."

—Malachi 3:8–12

"WHY SHOULD I TITHE?"

Why should we tithe? We should tithe because the Bible teaches it. We accept the Bible's teachings about salvation, divine healing, God's provision, and mansions in heaven. Therefore, we must accept the Bible's teaching of tithing as well. It's from the same Book, inspired by the same Holy Spirit—who is God!

Tithing is recorded in the Old Testament.

You may say, "Tithing was taught under the Law, and the Law has been done away with." Wrong! Tithing was taught in the Bible four hundred thirty years *before* the Law was given. Tithing is not a dispensational principle; *it's a divine principle*.

Abraham paid tithes to Melchizedek four hundred thirty years before the Law.

> Then Melchizedek king of Salem brought out bread and wine; he was the priest of God Most High. And he blessed him and said: "Blessed be Abram of God Most High, possessor of heaven and earth; and blessed be God Most High, who has delivered your enemies into your hand." And he [Abraham] gave him [Melchizedek] a tithe of all.
>
> —Genesis 14:18–20

When Jacob was at Bethel and saw a vision of angels ascending and descending on a ladder into heaven, He said to God, "And this stone which I have set as a pillar shall be God's house, and of all that You give me I will surely give a tenth to You" (Gen. 28:22). Jacob said he would give "a tenth," which equals *a tithe*.

And we read in Leviticus 27:30:

> And all the tithe of the land, whether of the seed of the land or of the fruit of the tree, is the LORD's. It is holy to the LORD.

How much of the tithe belongs to the Lord? All of it! Not 5 percent...not 8 percent...not *divine tipping,* but 10 percent belongs to the Lord. In fact, when you stop to think, *all* of it belongs to God! He is only asking for one-tenth of it!

It is a historical fact that throughout the Old Testament, when God's people were in harmony with God—they tithed. As a result they prospered greatly and became wealthy.

In Genesis 13:2 we discover that Abraham was "very rich." And not just rich *spiritually*—he was rich in gold, in silver, and in cattle.

It is also a historical fact that when God's people did not tithe, God sent famine and drought to the land.

Jesus tithed.

Another reason we should tithe is because of the example Jesus set. Jesus tithed. He taught tithing in the New Testament.

> Woe to you, scribes and Pharisees, hypocrites! For you pay tithe of mint and anise and cummin, and have neglected the weightier matters of the law: justice and mercy and faith. These you ought to have done, without leaving the others undone.
>
> —MATTHEW 23:23

Peter taught the early church to give to God.

Peter taught the New Testament church to sell all they had and bring it to the church and lay it at the apostles' feet. Most of the people obeyed Peter's teaching, but Ananias and Sapphira *pretended to give everything* but kept some back for their own personal use. They lied about their contributions to the kingdom of God. And, as a result, God struck them dead.

Stop praying about prospering when you're stealing from God!

We should tithe because God is in control of everything.

God controls all the wealth in the world. He controls your health…your breath…your business…and your ability to get wealth—it's not real intelligent to provoke God!

If you choose not to tithe, "Poverty and shame will come to him who disdains correction" (Prov. 13:18).

GOD OR MAMMON?

The reason God asks you to tithe is to give you the opportunity to prove that you are not living in idolatry. Matthew 6:24 admonishes, "No one can serve two masters; for either he will hate the one and love the other, or else he will be loyal to the one and despise the other. You cannot serve God and mammon."

Mammon is world wealth. It is a personification of wealth and greed as a false god. Mammon was a Syrian god of riches.

God asks you to give what is dear to you. If you love your money more than God, He'll take it from you. Giving is proof that greed does not control you.

We see this principle illustrated in the life of Abraham. God said to Abraham, "Prove that you love me by giving me the one thing that is dearest to you—your only son." Abraham passed the test of giving by his willingness to sacrifice Isaac on the altar. (See Genesis 22.)

Once Abraham had shown God his willingness to give his son, God said to Abraham, "Now let Me show you what I will give to you."

> Then the Angel of the Lord called to Abraham a second time out of heaven, and said: "By Myself I have sworn, says the Lord, because you have done this thing, and have not withheld your son, your only son—blessing I will bless you, and in multiplying I will multiply your descendants as the stars of the heaven and as the sand which is on the seashore; and your descendants shall possess the gate of their enemies. In your seed all the nations of the earth shall be blessed, because you have obeyed My voice."
>
> —Genesis 22:15–18

Abraham did not get his inheritance until he demonstrated that he was willing and obedient to give. Then God gave him the Promised Land flowing with milk and honey, and made him the spiritual father of all who believe.

God gives the same promise of blessing to all who obey His command to give. He told the Hebrews, "So it shall be, when the LORD your God brings you into the land of which He swore to your fathers, to Abraham, Isaac, and Jacob, to give you large and beautiful cities which you did not build, houses full of all good things, which you did not fill, hewn-out wells which you did not dig, vineyards and olive trees which you did not plant..." (Deut. 6:10–11).

In other words, God was saying, "I'll cause prosperity to run over you like a Mack truck!" But the commandment is this: Tithe first. Give your best to God first; give Him your firstfruits.

This is how the New Testament says it: "But seek first the kingdom of God and His righteousness, and all these things shall be added to you" (Matt. 6:33).

If you will obey God's commandment to tithe, you will not live under an economic curse. In Malachi 3:9, God said, "You are cursed with a curse, for you have robbed Me." I didn't say that—God did!

If you have found yourself on an economic treadmill, working harder and harder for less and less, *are you tithing?* If you never seem to have enough...and every time you try to make ends meet, it seems that God moves the middle—*are you tithing?*

If you are not tithing, your business is under a curse. God will not allow you to prosper because you are living contrary to His Word. God calls you a thief and a robber if you do not give to Him what belongs to Him. Remember what the prophet Haggai said (Hag. 1:6).

But when you tithe, God rebukes the devourer (Satan) for your sake.

> "And I will rebuke the devourer for your sakes,
> So that he will not destroy the fruit of your ground,

Nor shall the vine fail to bear fruit for you in the field,"
Says the LORD of hosts.

—MALACHI 3:11

In the current economic crisis America is facing, remember that God is in control. He is not in heaven wringing His hands. He's not saying, "Let's make a deal." He is in heaven saying, "*This is the deal!*"

It is God's plan to secure your financial freedom. The money you spend on lunch will last about four hours. The money you spend for a new car will last about thirty-six months. But the money you spend for the kingdom of God *will last forever*.

Chapter 12

THE POWER TO GET WEALTH

T HIS CHAPTER PRESENTS THE PRINCIPLE OF *FARMING* YOUR way to financial freedom. No, I'm not suggesting that everyone move out of the city to the farmlands, build a barn, buy some livestock, plant some corn, and wear a hat that says, "I'm a farmer."

I want you to understand the importance of doing what farmers do. I want you to learn to plant your spiritual seed for the harvest that God will bring to you. An ancient poet said, "He who plants a seed becomes a partner with God."

> And you shall remember the LORD your God, for it is
> He who gives you power to get wealth.
> —DEUTERONOMY 8:18

FARM YOUR WAY TO FINANCIAL FREEDOM

Everything that God does on Earth comes from a seed.

> While the earth remains,
> Seedtime and harvest,
> Cold and heat,
> Winter and summer,
> And day and night
> Shall not cease.
> —GENESIS 8:22

Consider this principle in the spiritual realm for a moment. How did Jesus Christ come to Earth? The answer is that He came according to the principle of seedtime and harvest.

> And I will put enmity between you and the woman, and
> between your seed and her Seed; He shall bruise your
> head, and you shall bruise His heel.
>
> —GENESIS 3:15

The Holy Spirit planted a Seed into Mary's womb, and the kingdom of Satan was defeated. As a result, demons tremble at the mention of the name of Jesus. Through this Seed—Jesus Christ—we have salvation, healing, and deliverance. We have love, joy, peace, and power to walk in victory because of seedtime and harvest.

But consider the physical realm also. How did you get here? You also were brought to life through the principle of seedtime and harvest. Those two events were separated by nine months.

Consider also the financial realm. We have already learned the principle of Luke 6:38:

> Give, and it will be given to you: good measure, pressed
> down, shaken together, and running over will be put
> into your bosom. For with the same measure that you
> use, it will be measured back to you.

Become *seed* conscious, not *need* conscious.

We must learn to become *seed* conscious, not *need* conscious. Every time God gives you an opportunity to give, He's giving you an opportunity to increase your income. You can *farm* your way to financial freedom by planting your seed in good ground.

In Matthew 13:3–8, Jesus told the story of the sower.

> Then He spoke many things to them in parables, saying:
> "Behold, a sower went out to sow. And as he sowed,
> some seed fell by the wayside; and the birds came and
> devoured them. Some fell on stony places, where they
> did not have much earth; and they immediately sprang
> up because they had no depth of earth. But when the
> sun was up they were scorched, and because they had no
> root they withered away. And some fell among thorns,
> and the thorns sprang up and choked them. But others
> fell on good ground and yielded a crop: some a hundred-
> fold, some sixty, some thirty."

Just as with that sower, God increases our seed and gives us a harvest greater than what we plant. It may be thirtyfold, sixtyfold, or a hundredfold.

In the late 1970s, Diana and I purchased a 130-acre farm. It was beautiful, and we planned to keep it all our lives. But there came a time when our television ministry needed the money, so we decided to sow our farm into world evangelism.

Did it come back? Oh, yes. Four years ago our farm came back to us as a beautiful ranch. The return was exactly sixtyfold.

You may be so far behind financially that you don't believe it is possible to ever catch up. But you are wrong.

> And God is able to make all grace (every favor and earthly blessing) come to you in abundance, so that you may always and under all circumstances and whatever the need be self-sufficient [possessing enough to require no aid or support and furnished in abundance for every good work and charitable donation].
>
> —2 CORINTHIANS 9:8, AMP

Notice this important principle in the verse: God is willing and able to make it up to you. He can give you back what the enemy has stolen from you. He can give back what you may have lost in bankruptcy or what you lost in a business failure. He can give back what you lost when you were unemployed.

Write down your financial plan, be prudent in the decisions you make, be diligent in executing your plan, and even though it may tarry, your plan will come. "Then the LORD answered me and said: 'Write the vision and make it plain on tablets, that he may run who reads it'" (Hab. 2:2).

Your only hope of catching up lies in your willingness to plant your seed in the kingdom of God.

You must plant your seed before you can expect an increase.

Without seedtime, it's impossible to have harvest time. If you give nothing…you get nothing. God can increase what you give a hundredfold. But nothing times nothing equals nothing! In John 12:24, Jesus said, "Most assuredly, I say to you, unless a grain of wheat falls into the ground and dies, it remains alone; but if it dies, it produces much grain."

When what you have in your hand is not enough to meet your need, it's your seed! You can do three things with seed:

1. Eat it.
2. Feed it to your cows.
3. Plant it!

There is no chance of increase until you plant it. Choose to plant your seed. You may think that you have nothing to give, but that is not correct.

> Now may He who supplies seed to the sower, and bread for food, supply and multiply the seed you have sown and increase the fruits of your righteousness, while you are enriched in everything for all liberality, which causes thanksgiving through us to God.
> —2 CORINTHIANS 9:10–11

You may not feel as if you understand God's economic system, but you don't have to understand it for it to work. I don't understand how a black cow eats green grass and gives white milk and yellow butter. But I still drink milk and eat butter—and enjoy both!

We simply cannot know everything that God knows. It's enough to know that we can trust what He says to us!

> "For My thoughts are not your thoughts,
> Nor are your ways My ways," says the LORD.
> "For as the heavens are higher than the earth,
> So are My ways higher than your ways,
> And My thoughts than your thoughts."
> —ISAIAH 55:8–9

When you plant your seed in the kingdom of God, God multiplies it far better than Wall Street. Wall Street has gone broke in the past, but the needs of God's children have never challenged the riches of His kingdom. Your investments are being administered by Jehovah-Jireh. He provided a cloud by day and fire by night to guide the Hebrews to the Promised Land. He provided them with manna and kept them from illness. He fed Elijah in the midst of famine, and He can provide for you.

You determine the size of your harvest when you sow your seed.

Do you need a barn-bursting harvest? Then sow lots of seed. "He who sows sparingly will also reap sparingly, and he who sows bountifully will also reap bountifully" (2 Cor. 9:6).

PLANT YOUR SEED IN GOOD GROUND

God wants us to plant our seed in good ground. Good ground means the kingdom of God. Be aware that not every church or ministry or television ministry or charitable organization is *good ground*. Be sure that the places where you plant your seed are true and accurate representations of the kingdom of God.

When a church ordains homosexuals into gospel ministry, it does not represent the kingdom of God (Rom. 1:27). If a ministry denies the Virgin Birth (Isa. 7:4; Matt. 1:23–25) or denies that the Bible is the inspired Word of God (2 Tim. 3:16), it is not *good ground*. If it supports abortion, Jesus said, "I have come that they may have life, and that they may have it more abundantly" (John 10:10). Abortion is death, and any church or organization that supports abortion is not representative of the kingdom of God.

LEARN TO BE PATIENT— YOU MUST WAIT FOR THE HARVEST

The process of seedtime and harvest takes patience. God tell us that it is through "faith and patience" that we inherit the promises (Heb. 6:12). In God's teaching on sowing, He said the following about good ground: "But the ones that fell on the good ground are those who, having heard the word with a noble and good heart, keep it and bear fruit with patience" (Luke 8:15).

Hebrews 10:36 says, "For ye have need of patience, that, after ye have done the will of God, ye might receive the promise" (KJV). You can plant your seed—and do it abundantly in good ground. But you can still kill your harvest if you lack patience.

Esau sold his birthright for a bowl of pottage because of impatience. His impatience killed his harvest (Gen. 25:32)!

If you invest a thousand dollars in the kingdom of God by placing a check in the offering plate on Sunday morning, don't look for your hundredfold return before you get to the lobby. Impatience will kill your harvest.

You can also kill your harvest by murmuring, negative, toxic words as you wait *impatiently* for your harvest (Num. 16:41). Murmuring sounds like this:

- "God's not going to come through this time."
- "I've waited long enough."
- "Where is God when I really need Him?"

When Israel murmured against God, He sent snakes to bite them (Num. 21:6). Remember that the snake is a symbol of Satan (Gen. 3:1). When you murmur, you are inviting snakes to enter your life, your family, your business, and your church. You're permitting Satan to destroy your harvest.

GOD'S PROVISION IS IN HIS PROMISES

You can find God's *provision* in His *promises*. Remember this: *there is abundant wealth in the Word.*

> Grace and peace be multiplied unto you through the knowledge of God, and of Jesus our Lord, according as his divine power hath given unto us all things that pertain unto life and godliness, through the knowledge of him that hath called us to glory and virtue: Whereby are given unto us exceeding great and precious promises: that by these ye might be partakers of the divine nature, having escaped the corruption that is in the world through lust.
> —2 Peter 1:2–4, kjv

These verses proclaim that grace and peace are multiplied. The Christian life is not stagnant—it begins with *great* and gets *better*! How? Through "the knowledge of him that hath called us to glory and virtue: Whereby are given unto us exceeding great and precious promises." Your inheritance is found in the precious promises of God's Word, and He is the ultimate promise keeper.

As you come into the knowledge of God's Word and act upon His promises (faith), His abundance (wealth) becomes yours.

The $64,000 question is this: Will you act on God's Word and be given the power to get wealth, or will you continue whining in the wilderness and receive nothing? The choice is yours.

What is *legally yours* and what is *literally yours* are very different in the Bible. Your wealth is assured in Scripture. But it's not yours until you act on it!

In the Old Testament, Joshua brought Israel into the Promised Land (Josh. 4). In the New Testament, Jesus brought the church into the land of promises—the Word of God.

Israel's first victory *en route* to the Promised Land was via a miracle—the supernatural victory of the walls of Jericho falling down. (See Joshua 6.) Every other victory came by violent combat—Israel had to take action and fight for every inch of the territory!

Let me give you the Hagee translation of that principle. Jesus Christ has led every one of us into the wealth of the kingdom of God. You came into the kingdom of God through the supernatural miracle of redemption. Thereafter your victories come through supernatural warfare.

God will be your defender, your fortress, your shield, your buckler, and your high tower, but according to St. Paul's teaching, you still have to put on the whole armor of God and "fight the good fight" (Eph. 6:11–13).

Don't sit on your blessed assurance and tell God to send in the harvest. Go get it! He provides worms for birds, but He doesn't throw the worms down their throats. Don't say, "God will just give it to me." If you are not willing to fight the giants, you don't get to eat the grapes or drink of the milk and honey.

Your provision lies within God's promises, but you will have to activate those promises by taking action as God directs you. You have all the tools you need to avoid a personal economic crash in the midst of the world's economic collapse. Follow the advice, counsel, and direction of our Master Investment

Counselor. Using your Manual—the Word of God—is all you need to know how to forge ahead into financial freedom and divine prosperity.

AN ENCOURAGING WORD

In this climate of great global unrest, have confidence in God. You and I did nothing to create this crisis and unrest; therefore, if we are following God's economic system in His Word, we have nothing to fear. God is on the throne—and He protects His own.

> The steps of a good man are ordered by the LORD,
> And He delights in his way.
> Though he fall, he shall not be utterly cast down;
> For the LORD upholds him with His hand.
> I have been young, and now am old;
> Yet I have not seen the righteous forsaken,
> Nor his descendants begging bread.
> He is ever merciful, and lends;
> And his descendants are blessed.
> —PSALM 37:23–26

Notes

Foreword

1. The Avalon Project at Yale Law School, "First Inaugural Address of Franklin D. Roosevelt," March 4, 1933, http://www.yale.edu/lawweb/avalon/presiden/inaug/froos1.htm (accessed October 10, 2008).

2. Larry Bates, *The New Economic Disorder* (Lake Mary, FL: Excel Books, 2008), 10.

1—What Is Going On?

1. David Herszenhorn, "Bailout Plan Wins Approval; Democrats Vow Tighter Rules," *New York Times*, October 3, 2008, http://www.nytimes.com/2008/10/04/business/economy/04bailout.html?bl&ex=1223265600&en=80352c05b6d4b135&ei=5087 (accessed October 5, 2008).

2. Associated Press, "2nd LD: 6 Central Banks, Including Fed, ECB, Cut Interest Rates," October 8, 2008, http://www.breitbart.com/article.php?id=D93MAHTG0&show_article=1 (accessed October 9, 2008).

3. Bates, *The New Economic Disorder*, 10.

4. Ibid., 16–22.

5. Bill Wilson, "US Using New Banking Powers to Establish Prophetic New World Order," *The Daily Jot With Bill Wilson*, October 8, 2008, http://www.dailyjot.com/news_379.html (accessed October 10, 2008).

6. Jeannine Aversa, "Fed Slashes Interest Rates, but Stocks Lose Again," Associated Press, October 9, 2008, http://ap.google.com/article/ALeqM5ioHc80xKMiATnqCpK0cDKJzk_nPQD93MON0O0 (October 10, 2008).

2—The Economic Meltdown: the Perfect Storm

1. The research for the material in this chapter was completed by David A. Crockett, PhD.

2. David M. Smick, *The World Is Curved: Hidden Dangers to the Global Economy* (New York: Penguin, 2008), 16–18.

3. Jeannine Aversa, Associated Press, October 11, 2008.

4. Dave Carpenter, Associated Press, October 9, 2008.

5. Joseph E. Stiglitz, "The Dismal Questions," *New York Times*, October 7, 2008.

6. Mark Zandi, *Financial Shock: A 360° Look at the Subprime Mortgage Implosion, and How to Avoid the Next Financial Crisis* (Upper Saddle River, NJ: FT Press, 2009), 168.

7. Burton W. Folsom Jr., "Financial Crisis—Yes; Great Depression—No," John M. Ashbrook Center for Public Affairs, September 2008; Gary S. Becker, "We're Not Headed for a Depression," *Wall Street Journal*, October 7, 2008.

8. John Steele Gordon, "A Short Banking History of the United States: Why Our System Is Prone to Panics," *Wall Street Journal*, October 10, 2008.

9. Zandi, *Financial Shock*, 45.

10. Ibid., 31.

11. Robert J. Shiller, *The Subprime Solution: How Today's Global Financial Crisis Happened, and What to Do about It* (Princeton, NJ: Princeton University Press, 2008), 48–49; Zandi, *Financial Shock*, 65–72.

12. Shiller, *The Subprime Solution*, 32.

13. Zandi, *Financial Shock*, 9.

14. Ibid., 35–40.

15. Shiller, *The Subprime Solution*, 41–47; Smick, *The World Is Curved*, 206–207; Zandi, *Financial Shock*, 61–62.

16. Smick, *The World Is Curved*, 245–247.

17. Shiller, *The Subprime Solution*, 34–38; Zandi, *Financial Shock*, 166–167.

18. Smick, *The World Is Curved*, 248.

19. Zandi, *Financial Shock*, 81–88; Shiller, *The Subprime Solution*, 63.

20. Smick, *The World Is Curved*, 95–115.

21. Ibid., 57–59.

22. Zandi, *Financial Shock*, 220–221, 231–232; Smick, *The World Is Curved*, 50–55, 191.

23. Smick, *The World Is Curved*, 156, 225–226.

24. *The Federal Government's Financial Health: A Citizen's Guide to the 2007 Financial Report of the United States Government.*

25. Shiller, *The Subprime Solution*, 102–103; Zandi, *Financial Shock*, 214–227.

26. David A. Crockett, *Running Against the Grain: How Opposition Presidents Win the White House* (College Station, TX: Texas A&M University Press, 2008).

27. Shiller, *The Subprime Solution*, 25.

28. David Brooks, "Big Government Ahead," *New York Times,* October 14, 2008.

3—The Rise and Fall of America

1. Personal journal of George Washington, as quoted in Newt Gingrich, *Winning the Future: A 21st Century Contract With America* (Washington DC: Regnery Publishers, 2005), 200. According to the Valley Forge FAQs site of USHistory.org, the date of the journal entry was September 17, 1796, http://www.ushistory.org/valle yforge/youasked/060.htm (accessed October 9, 2008).

2. As quoted in Andrew Kohut and Bruce Stokes, *America Against the World: How We Are Different and Why We Are Disliked* (New York: Henry Holt and Company, LLC, 2006), 100.

3. John Wesley Hill, *Abraham Lincoln, Man of God* (New York: Putnam's Sons, 1920), 257.

4. FOXNews.com, "Flap After Court Rules Pledge of Allegiance Unconstitutional," June 27, 2002, http://www.foxnews.com/story/0,2933,56310,00 .html (accessed October 3, 2008).

5. Statistic released by the Centers for Disease Control in November 2005, quoted in Rev. John J. Raphael, SSJ, "Silent No More: A Major Crisis in the African American Community," The National Black Catholic Congress, http://www.nbcco ngress.org/features/abortion_silent_no_more_01.asp (accessed October 3, 2008).

6. Peggy Noonan, "A Separate Peace: America Is in Trouble—and Our Elites Are Merely Resigned," *Wall Street Journal*, October 2005, cited in *Peak Oil: Crisis and Catalyst for a Sustainable Future*, an Oberlin Experimental College Course

online at http://www.sfbayoil.org/sfpc/media/Peak_Oil_ExCo_Commentary.pdf (accessed October 3, 2008).

7. UCLA Asian American Studies Center, "U.S./China Media Brief: U.S.-China Trade Imbalance," http://www.aasc.ucla.edu/uschina/trade_tradeimbalance .shtml (accessed October 3, 2008).

8. Tony Halpin, "Russia Ratchets Up US tensions With Arms Sales to Iran and Venezuela," *Times Online*, September 19, 2008, http://www.timesonline.co.uk/tol/ news/world/europe/article4781027.ece (accessed October 3, 2008).

9. "Ahmadinejad: Israel a 'Stinking Corpse,'" *Jerusalem Post*, May 8, 2008, http://www.jpost.com/servlet/Satellite?cid=1209627040670&pagename=JPost%2FJ PArticle%2FShowFull (accessed October 17, 2008).

10. "Congress Set to Adjourn Without Passing New Iran Sanctions," *niacIN-sight*, http://niacblog.wordpress.com/2008/09/23/congress-set-to-adjourn -without-passing-new-iran-sanctions/ (accessed October 17, 2008).

11. Wikipedia.org, "List of Terrorist Incidents," 2002–2008, http://en.wikipedia .org/wiki/List_of_terrorist_incidents,_2002 (accessed October 18, 2008).

12. For more information about *hudna*, see "Hudnawatch: The Meaning of Hudna and the Rain of Qassams," http://www.zionism-israel.com/log/ archives/00000329.html (accessed October 4, 2008).

13. Florence C. Fee, "Russia and Iraq: the Question of the Russian Oil Contracts," *Middle East Economic Survey*, http://www.mees.com/postedarticles/ oped/a46n14d01.htm (accessed October 18, 2008).

14. Abdelaziz L. Al-Khalifat, "Dead Sea Rate of Evaporation, *American Journal of Applied Sciences* (August 2008): http://findarticles.com/p/articles/mi_7109/is_/ ai_n28552360 (accessed October 18, 2008).

15. HistoryCommons.org, "May 2006: FEMA Warns of Nuclear 'Suitcase Bombs,'" http://www.historycommons.org/context.jsp?item=FemaSuitNukes (accessed October 4, 2008).

16. Aneki.com, "Largest Christian Populations in the World," referencing *CIA Factbook*, http://www.aneki.com/christian.html (accessed October 4, 2008).

4—A Fight for World Control

1. AFP.Google.com, "Ahmadinejad Says Israel Will Soon Disappear," June 2, 2008, http://afp.google.com/article/ALeqM5gkqvlPndHPxXMqNzQLCQAPNyxb dQ (accessed October 2, 2008).

2. Aljazeera.net, "Ahmadinejad: Wipe Israel Off Map," October 26, 2005, http://english.aljazeera.net/archive/2005/10/200849132648612154.html (accessed October 9, 2008).

3. Jahangir Arasli, "Obsolete Weapons, Unconventional Tactics, and Martyrdom Zeal: How Iran Would Apply Its Asymmetric Naval Warfare Doctrine in a Future Conflict," *Storming Media Pentagon Reports*, April 2007, http://www .stormingmedia.us/35/3588/A358874.html (accessed October 3, 2008).

4. Kenneth R. Timmerman, "U.S. Intel: Iran Plans Nuclear Strike on U.S.," NewsMax.com, July 29, 2008, http://www.newsmax.com/timmerman/iran_ nuclear_plan/2008/07/29/117217.html (accessed October 2, 2008).

5. John Hagee, *Jerusalem Countdown* (Lake Mary, FL: FrontLine, 2006), 63–64.

6. Timmerman, "U.S. Intel: Iran Plans Nuclear Strike on U.S."

7. Reuters.com, "FACTBOX-Foreign Investment in Iran From 2000–2007," January 16, 2008, http://www.reuters.com/article/BROKER/idUSL1684472920080116 (accessed October 2, 2008).

8. Shmuel Rosner, "U.S. Campaign Calls for Major U.S. Divestment," Haaretz .com, March 13, 2007 http://www.haaretz.com/hasen/spages/836468.html (accessed October 2, 2008).

9. Craig Karmin, "Pension Funds Gain Leeway on Terror Laws," *Wall Street Journal*, April 15, 2008, http://online.wsj.com/article/SB120821970179614679.html (accessed October 2, 2008).

10. The Strait of Hormuz, leading out of the Persian Gulf, is one of the two most strategic chokepoints for world oil. For more information, see Energy Information Administration, "World Oil Transit Chokepoints," http://www.eia .doe.gov/cabs/World_Oil_Transit_Chokepoints/Background.html (accessed October 3, 2008).

11. Zogby.com, "Zogby Poll: 74% Support Off-shore Drilling in U.S. Coastal Waters," June 20, 2008, http://www.zogby.com/news/ReadNews.dbm?ID=1519 (accessed October 3, 2008).

12. Mike Lillis, "Democrats Cave on Off-shore Drilling," *The Washington Independent*, September 24, 2008, http://washingtonindependent.com/7339/democrats-cave-big-on-offshore-drilling (accessed October 3, 2008).

13. Paul Vercammen, "Diesel Thieves Wreak Havoc on California farmers," CNN.com, June 5, 2008, http://www.cnn.com/2008/US/06/05/stealing.fuel/index .html#cnnSTCText (accessed October 3, 2008).

14. David Dickson, "Former Oil Exec: Gas Rationing Needed," *Washington Times*, September 15, 2008, http://www.washingtontimes.com/news/2008/sep/15/gas-rationing-needed-former-oil-executive-says/ (accessed October 3, 2008).

15. Michael Kanellos, "The Biofuel Factor in Rising Food Prices," April 15, 2008, CNET.com, http://news.cnet.com/8301-11128_3-9918741-54.html (accessed October 3, 2008).

16. Lee Kaplan, "The Saudi Fifth Column on our Nation's Campuses," FrontPageMagazine.com, April 5, 2004, http://www.frontpagemag.com/Articles/Read.aspx?GUID=7634EF94-18DC-471C-A93F-6D0C0E15F610 (accessed October 3, 2008).

5—Rebirth of the Roman Empire: The European Union

1. Winston Churchill, from a speech given to academic youth given in Zurich, Switzerland, on September 19, 1946, http://www.coe.int/T/E/Com/About_Coe/DiscoursChurchill.asp (accessed October 4, 2008).

2. T. R. Reid, *The United States of Europe* (New York: Penguin Press, 2004).

6—Beginning the Road to Armageddon

1. Associated Press, "UN Atomic Agency to Probe Whether Syria Has Secret Nuclear Program," CBC.com, June 22, 2008, http://www.cbc.ca/world/story/2008/06/22/un-syria.html (accessed October 2, 2008).

2. Hagee, *Jerusalem Countdown*, 138.

3. "The Organization of Islamic Conference Member States (OIC)," Infoplease, http://www.infoplease.com/spot/oicstates1.html (accessed October 18, 2008).

4. Sala@m.com, "Muslims in the West," Sala@m, http://www.salaam.co.uk/themeofthemonth/april02_index.php (accessed October 3, 2008).

7—Has World War III Begun?

1. JPost.com Staff, "Ahmadinejad: Israel Will Disappear," JerusalemPost.com, December 2, 2006, http://www.jpost.com/servlet/Satellite?pagename=JPost%2FJPArticle%2FShowFull&cid=1164881801325 (accessed October 4, 2008).

2. Mary Jordan, "Britain MI5 Warns of Rising Terror Threat," WashingtonPost.com, November 11, 2006, http://www.washingtonpost.com/wp-dyn/content/article/2006/11/10/AR2006111000138.html (accessed October 4, 2008).

3. Hagee, *Jerusalem Countdown*, 63–65.

4. "Ahmadinejad Says Israel Will Soon Disappear," June 2, 2008, breitbart.com, http://www.breitbart.com/article.php?id=080602124328.f6eyi8y1&show_article=1 (accessed October 18, 2008).

5. Daniel Pipes, "At War With Islamic Fascists," FrontPageMagazine.com, August 14, 2006, cited on Middle East Forum, http://www.meforum.org/article/pipes/3848 (accessed October 4, 2008).

6. Sasha Nagy, "Massive Terror Attack Averted: RCMP," GlobeandMail.com, June 3, 2006, http://www.theglobeandmail.com/servlet/story/RTGAM.20060603.wwarrants0603_3/BNStory/National/home (accessed October 4, 2008).

7. BBCNews.com, "Scores Die in Madrid Bomb Carnage," March 11, 2004, http://news.bbc.co.uk/1/hi/world/europe/3500452.stm (accessed October 4, 2008).

8. Farhan Bokhari, "China to Help Pakistan Build 2 Nuke Plants," CBSNews.com, October 18, 2008, http://www.cbsnews.com/stories/2008/10/18/world/printable4530697.shtml (accessed October 18, 2008).

9. Robin Wright, *Sacred Rage: The Wrath of Militant Islam* (New York: Simon and Schuster, 1985), 99.

10. For one example of these reports, see "Murder in the Family: Honor Killings in America," FoxNews.com, July 26, 2008, http://www.foxnews.com/story/0,2933,391531,00.html (accessed October 4, 2008).

11. David Brockman, "Death of a Princess," Behind the Scenes, July 2, 2005, http://www.transdiffusion.org/emc/behindthescreens/princess.php (accessed October 4, 2008).

12. Dave Hunt, *Judgment Day! Islam, Israel, and the Nations* (Bend, OR: The Berean Call, 2006).

13. Ibid.

14. Kenneth R. Timmerman, "Protest Rap Sheet: Saudi Official Should Look to Saudi Clerics Before Blasting Gen. Boykin," commentary from Sunday, October 6, 2003, http://www.kentimmerman.com/2003_10_26jubeir-boykin (accessed October 4, 2008).

15. Ibid.

16. Winston Churchill's first speech as prime minister, "Blood, Toil, Tears and Sweat," May 13, 1940, The Churchill Centre, http://www.winstonchurchill.org/i4a/pages/index.cfm?pageid=391 (accessed October 4, 2008).

8—What Do I Do Now?

1. Albert Mohler, "A Christian View of the Economic Crisis," AlbertMohler .com, http://www.albertmohler.com/blog_read.php?id=2550 (accessed October 6, 2008).

9—Prosperity Is a Choice

1. For more on the story of the Rothschilds, see Paul Vallely, "The Rothschild Story: A Golden Era Ends for a Secretive Dynasty," *The Independent*, April 16, 2004, http://www.independent.co.uk/news/uk/this-britain/the-rothschild-story-a-golden-era-ends-for-a-secretive-dynasty-756388.html (accessed October 5, 2008).

2. Betsy Stark, "Understanding the Financial Crisis and Bailout," *Money Beat*, September 25, 2008, http://blogs.abcnews.com/moneybeat/2008/09/understanding -t.html (accessed October 5, 2008).

3. "Market's 7-Day Rout Leaves U.S. Reeling," *Wall Street Journal*, October 10, 2008, http://online.wsj.com/article/SB122359593027021243.html (accessed October 21, 2008).

4. "While the World Is Listening, Brown Touts Global Oversight," *Wall Street Journal*, October 15, 2008, http://online.wsj.com/article/SB122401864921433845 .html (accessed October 21, 2008).

5. Ben W. (bdarbs), "Mass Foreclosures Threaten the U.S.," *EFinance Directory*, July 12, 2007, http://efinancedirectory.com/articles/Mass_Foreclosures_Threaten_ the_U.S..html (accessed October 5, 2008).

6. "U.S. National Debt Clock, accessed at http://www.brillig.com/debt_clock/.

7. Brian Fallow, "One-in-Four Chance of Global Recession Out of US Crisis," *New Zealand Herald*, April 11, 2008, http://www.nzherald.co.nz/business/news/ article.cfm?c_id=3&objectid=10503438 (accessed October 8, 2008).

8. "NYC National Debt Clock runs out of digits," Newsday.com, http://www .newsday.com/news.local/wire/newyork/ny-bc-ny--nationaldeb tclock1008oct08,0,3534534.story.

10—Givers Gain

1. Bill G. Page, *Making Money Work* (n.p.: Willie Glen Page, Inc., 2005).

2. "He Paid a Debt He Did Not Owe" by Ellis J. Crum. Copyright © 1977 in *Special Sacred Selections* by Ellis J. Crum, publisher, Kendallville, IN 46755. International copyright secured. All rights reserved. Used by permission.